AF801245

Oklahoma Automobile Insurance Law and Practice

2012 Supplement

By:
Brad Smith, Esq.
The Barkley Law Firm
Tulsa, Oklahoma

Redbud Publishing Co.
4711 W. 88th St., Tulsa Oklahoma 74132

COPYRIGHT © 1996, 1999, 2004, 2012
By Brad Smith
First Printing 1996, Second Printing 1999,Third Printing 2004
Fourth Printing 2012

All rights reserved. No part of this book may be reproduced or transmitted in any form or by any means, electronic or mechanical, including photocopying, recording or by any information storage and retrieval system without written permission from the author, except for the inclusion of brief quotations in a review.

Printed in the United States of America.
Published by Redbud Publishing Co., 4711 W. 88th St., Tulsa, Oklahoma 74132.
Telephone: (918) 760-9733.

www.Redbudpub.com

ISBN-13 978-0-96532-420-5

About the Author

Brad Smith is a native of Tulsa, Oklahoma and a 1977 graduate of the University of Tulsa School of Law. He has had extensive experience in the field of insurance law, representing both insurers and insureds, Plaintiff and Defendant. His practice has encompassed all aspects of tort and insurance contract law, including automobile, general liability, commercial liability, trucker's policies and fire policies. He also handles appeals on various civil issues in Oklahoma and Federal Courts. Mr. Smith is with The Barkley Law Firm, and accepts referrals on insurance related cases and appeals, and does consultation, for both Plaintiffs and Defendants.

Brad Smith, Attorney at Law
The Barkley Law Firm
2700 Mid-Continent Tower
401 S. Boston Ave.
Tulsa, Oklahoma 74103-4035
Telephone: (918) 599-9991
Email: briefer@cox.net or
bsmith@thebarkleylawfirm.com

Preface
And Instructions for the Use of this Book

This is the update volume for Oklahoma Automobile Insurance Law and Practice. It must be read in conjunction with the main volume, which is available separately.

This book was written to aid the practicing lawyer, and insurance professional, in navigating the slippery and ever-changing slopes of Oklahoma automobile insurance law. Those practitioners already well versed in this area of law will find this a helpful reference and memory jogger. Those who are new to the area, or who only dabble infrequently, can use this as an "equalizer" to help them deal with their seasoned opponents.

But several levels of disclaimer are in order. My professional experience has included the representation of both the insurer and the insured. Like anyone else, I have developed attitudes and biases that may be reflected in my writing. I have genuinely attempted to keep unnecessary opinion out of the book. When an expression of opinion has been necessary, in order to explain a case, or warn the practitioner of a pitfall, I have tried to clearly label it as such.

This is only a guidebook. That means that the reader does not hold in his hands all there is to know about this subject. It would be proper for the reader to begin his legal research, or quest for understanding, by reading the appropriate section in this book. However, the reader would be remiss if she stopped here. This book can only give the reader a rough approximation of the past state of the law; it can not predict the future. Neither can this book account for every change in statute, every possible fact combination, or every nuance of policy language. Cases that are discussed here may already be outdated because of other developments in the law. It is the reader's responsibility to supplement this research and independently judge the current status of the law, or to contact legal counsel who can do so.

Further, I do not pretend that my research has been exhaustive. The author is a scholar, but a practicing scholar. I invite comments, criticisms and cases. If the reader believes that a subject has been treated unfairly, or that critical cases are missing, please contact me and I will make any needed changes. The book will be updated as needed. I also intend to expand the scope of the book to more fully cover some areas that need extended treatment.

I would like to acknowledge those professionals, in the Plaintiff and Defense Bar, who have helped and taught me since 1977. Those include, but are not limited to, Richard Gibbon, John Gladd, Sr., Joe Clark, Ray Wilburn and Gary Richardson, Fred Stoops, Tim Clancy and all of the associates with each of their firms. Special thanks to my friends at Taylor, Ryan, Schmidt, Van Dalsem & Williams, P.C., where my friend and mentor, Dennis King, taught me King's First Rule of Insurance Contract Interpretation: "Read the contract, stupid."

I also gratefully acknowledge Mike Barkley, and all my friends at The Barkley Law Firm, for giving me my current professional home.

I would also like to thank my family, and especially my wife Sue, for the love and support they have shown me and for putting up with my writing schedule. My mother, Norma Smith (RIP, 2001), gave many hours of invaluable professional proofreading assistance and advice, as well as words of encouragement. My father-in-law, Phil Sangunett (RIP, 2001), also offered many helpful words of encouragement.

Brad Smith, Esq.
The Barkley Law Firm
2700 Mid-Continent Tower
401 S. Boston Ave.
Tulsa, Okla. 74103-4035
Telephone: (918) 599-9991
Fax: (918) 584-1110
E-mail: briefer@cox.net or
bsmith@thebarkleylawfirm.com

Oklahoma Automobile Insurance
Law and Practice
-2012 Supplement

Updated and New Sections

Chapter 1: General Principles of Insurance.

§1:1 Introduction.

§1:2 Principles of Interpretation.

§1:7 -The "factual expectation test." When the insured does not have good title. The stolen vehicle problem.

Chapter 2: Definitions.

§2:2 "Named Insured," "You," "Your."

§2:6 -Accident: Was it an intentional act or injury?

§2:7 -Accident: Was it an accident from the insured's point of view?

§2:9 -Occurrence: At what point in time, or at what place, does an "occurrence" occur? Including issues of negligent entrustment or negligent supervision. [New]

§2:18 "Family Member" or "Relative"; "Resident

Chapter 3: General Contract Provisions and Conditions.

§3:38 –In General.

§3:47 - The relationship between "primary," "excess" and "escape" clauses.

§3:48 -What is other "similar insurance"?

§3:68 The Liability/UM Coverage "set-off" (reduction of amounts owed by tortfeasor because of payments made by UM insurer). [New]

§3:76 -Anti-stacking provisions.

§3:84 -Expiration of policy for Non-Payment.

§3:86 -Notice of Cancellation. Mailing and Receipt of Notice.

§3:87 Severability clauses. [New]

Chapter 4: Liability Coverage.

§4:3 The validity of the contract. Fraud and misrepresentation. [New]

§4:5 The insuring clause.

§4:7 -"Damages" or "All sums." Insurer's liability for punitive damages.

§4:11 – "Arising out of."

§4.12 – "Use" of a Motor Vehicle.

§4:34 -Use within the Scope of Consent of the Named Insured. Permissive Use. The Omnibus Clause.

§4:35 –The Omnibus Clause, In General.

§4:36 –Express Permission under the Omnibus Clause. "Second Permittee" Rules.

§4:45 - Non-traditional definitions of "insured."

§4:60 The Duty to Defend.

§4:61 -In General.

§4:62 -Control of the Defense and Settlement.

§4:65 -Duty Determined by the Allegations of the Petition or by the Facts Discoverable Through a Reasonable Investigation.

§4:68 The effect of exclusions held invalid under the Compulsory Liability Insurance Act. [New]

§4:70 -The Obligation of One Insurer to Contribute to Another for the Cost of Defending their Joint Insured.

§4:75 -The Obligation to Pay for Independent Counsel in a Conflict of Interest.

§4:80 The Duty to Settle

§4:81 -In General.

§4:88 - Prejudgment Interest.

§4:95 Compulsory Liability Insurance, Financial Responsibility and Out of State Coverage.

§4:97 -The effect of the Financial Responsibility Laws, including the Compulsory Liability Insurance Act, on the interpretation of insurance policies.

§4:99 –The effect of the CLIA on policy interpretation.

§4:103 The Plaintiff's failure to comply with the Compulsory Insurance Law. [New]

Chapter 5: Liability Coverage Exclusions.

§5:2 The Household and Named Insured Exclusion.

§5:3 Exclusion for "bodily injury and property damage caused intentionally by or at the direction of the insured."

§5:6 Care, Custody or Control Exclusion, or Property Which the Insured is "In Charge Of."

§5:7 The "Other Business" Exclusion.

§5:10 The named driver exclusion.

§5:15 Other Exclusions.

§5:16 Business Auto Policies: Operations Exclusion [new]

§5:17 Exclusions in homeowners and similar policies for use of a motor vehicle. [New]

Chapter 6: Uninsured Motorist Coverage.

§6:2 Applicability of the UM statute to certain "motor carrier" and "commercial" policies. [New]

§6:15 –The "underinsured" tortfeasor.

§6:17 The "self insured" tortfeasor as "uninsured motorist." [New]

§6:18 Allowing the statute of limitations to run against an otherwise insured tortfeasor does not make the tortfeasor "uninsured." [New]

§6:19 Settlement for less than tortfeasor's limits [New]

§6:30 Operation of motor vehicle and causation.

§6:32 Who is an Insured Person under Uninsured Motorist Coverage? Only an "insured person"

under a policy can claim the right to "stack" that policy.

§6:33 When is the insured "legally entitled to recover" against the uninsured motorist?

§6:35 What measure of damages can be recovered against the UM carrier?

§6:36 -Determining damages in relationship to available liability insurance. UM coverage as "primary." "Exhaustion" of liability coverage.

§6:38 -UM Coverage for Prejudgment Interest.

§6:42 The application and validity of exclusions in a UM policy.

§6:45 -Exclusion denying coverage when the insured takes a judgment against the tortfeasor, or sues the tortfeasor, without the consent of the UM insurer. The "no action' or "consent to sue" exclusion.

§6:49 -The named driver exclusion. [NEW]

§6:55 Limits of Liability.

§6:60 --The Workers Compensation set-off.

§6:65 Validity of provisions that reduce the limits of liability for certain insureds.

§6:70 The Other Insurance Clause. "Stacking" of UM coverages, and the "exhaustion" requirement.

§6:71 -In General.

§6.77 -Stacking. Fleet stacking.

§6:78 -The Limits of Stacking: The Payment of a Single Premium for coverage of Multiple Vehicles.

§6:79 -Requirement that the tortfeasor's liability insurance be "exhausted by payment" before the UM coverage is payable.

§6:80 -Primary UM vs Excess UM. The valid application of the "Other Insurance" provision and of the "exhaustion" requirement.

§6:94 –Keel v MFA and the four alternatives.

§6:96 –The UM insurer's obligation to evaluate the claim and make reasonable settlement offers.

§6:100 Subrogation and the Trust Agreement.

§6:101 -In General.

§6:102 - The destruction of subrogation rights by the insured's settlement with the tortfeasor. The "Porter Doctrine."

§6:105 -Protection of subrogation rights using the "substitute payment" provisions of §3636(E).

§7:17 Named Driver Exclusion.

Chapter 8: Property Coverages.

§8:25 The Measure of Damages. Limits of Liability; Actual cash value; repair; delay, etc.

§8:26 -In General

Oklahoma Automobile Insurance Law and Practice -2012 Supplement

Chapter 1: General Principles of Insurance.

§1:1 Introduction.

Other types of auto contracts as "insurance."

Oklahoma Courts have held that "gap protection" coverage, offered as an addendum to an auto loan, is "insurance," at least for purposes of the application of Oklahoma's bad faith law. *Embry v Innovative Aftermarket Systems*, 2008 OK CIV APP 92, 198 P.3d 388; on remand 2010 OK 82, 247 P.3d 1158.

Similarly, the Supreme Court held that some "vehicle service contracts" (extended warranty) meets the criteria for being "insurance" so that bad faith law would apply. *McMullan v Enterprise Financial Group, Inc.*, 2011 OK 7, 247 P.3d 1173. The reader should also review the Oklahoma Service Warranty Insurance Act, 36 O.S. §6601, et. seq., including the definition of "service warranty" in §6602.

§1:2 Principles of Interpretation.

In *Federal Ins. Co. v Tri-State Ins. Co.*, 157

F.3d 800 (10th Cir.1998) the Tenth Circuit held that "arise out of"language in a business auto policy exclusion should not be interpreted narrowly under the facts in that case, despite the fact that it was found in an exclusion. The "arising out of" language was in a coverage exclusion, and such exclusionary language is commonly interpreted narrowly (in favor of coverage). However, the Court said that, "Because we do not believe that we can make a principled distinction in meaning simply based upon where in the contract the phrase 'arising out of' appears, we decline to assign it a more restrictive meaning simply because it appears in the context of an exclusionary clause." *Id.* at 805.

For a case showing how the "reasonable expectations doctrine" (*Max True Plastering Co. v. USF & G Co.,* 1996 OK 28, 912 P.2d 861) is applied, see *Spears v Shelter Mutual Ins. Co.*, 2003 OK 66, 73 P.3d 865. The *Spears* case involves the interpretation of a homeowners policy.

Also see *American Economy Ins. Co. v Bogdahn*, 2004 OK 9, 89 P.3d 1051. The reasonable expectations doctrine may be applied only when: "(1) the challenged policy language is ambiguous, or (2) an exclusion within the policy is

(a) masked by technical or obscure language, or

(b) hidden in a policy's provisions."

The test for whether or not policy language is ambiguous is whether it "is susceptible to two interpretations on its face...from the standpoint of a reasonably prudent lay person, not from that of a lawyer." And, once an "ambiguity" is found, it will be construed against the insurer, and "Oklahoma now looks to the objectively reasonable expectations of the insured to fashion a remedy." ¶¶ 9-11.

Further, the Court held that policy language is not considered "ambiguous" simply because various courts disagree as to its interpretation. ¶ 20.

Once the parties to an insurance contract have agreed to its terms, courts are not free to rewrite the contract or make it better for either party. *Redcorn v State Farm Fire & Cas. Co.*, 2002 OK 15, 55 P.3d 1030.

In certain circumstances the terms of an insurance policy may violate public policy even if the policy does not violate the terms of a statute. *McElmurry v Garbow*, 2005 OK CIV APP 38, 116 P.3d 198.

An insurance policy is not "ambiguous" merely because two courts differ as to its interpretation, or because the parties disagree. Interpretation is a question of law for the court. *BP America, Inc. v State Auto Prop. & Cas. Ins. Co.*, 2005 OK 65, 148 P.3d 832. "Finally, payment of premiums is a crucial factor in determining whether a specific coverage is available to the insured." *Id.*

However, see *Haworth v Jantzen*, 2006 OK 35, 172 P.3d 193, discussed more fully in §2:26, where a perceived "ambiguity" between two phrases in the "motor vehicle" exclusion actually created coverage and turned a farm and ranch liability policy into an auto policy. One phrase unambiguously excluded coverage for motor vehicles. However, a second phrase excluded coverage for motor vehicles if the accident occurred away from the insured premises. The Court held that this created confusion (ambiguity) in the insured's mind, thus creating coverage.

Also see *Haberman v The Hartford Ins. Group*, 443 F.3d 1257 (10th Cir., 2006). The named insured on a Hartford commercial policy was a professional corporation. However, Haberman, the owner of the corporation, was listed by name, in a "Named Persons Endorsement." The Endorsement said that it "modifies insurance provided under the...Business Auto Coverage Form" and that Haberman is an "'insured' for Liability Coverage" under the "Liability Coverage" section of the policy. Haberman was involved in an accident in a friend's vehicle and made a UM claim against the Hartford policy. Hartford argued that the Endorsement extended coverage to Haberman individually only under the Liability policy. However, the Tenth Circuit held that the language of the Endorsement plainly extended Haberman coverage under the entire Business Auto Coverage, including UM or, in the alternative, was at least ambiguous and could be read to extend coverage to Haberman to the entire Business Auto Coverage, which would include UM. This case is also discussed in §§2:2, 6:32, and 6:77.

§1:7 -The "factual expectation test." When the insured does not have good title. The stolen vehicle problem.

Delk v Markel American Ins. Co., 2003 OK 88, 81 P.3d 629 involved the insurable interest of a cotenant in a home. This is a work emphasizing automobile insurance coverage, but the practitioner should review this case if issues arise regarding co-ownership in a vehicle.

Chapter 2: Definitions.

§2:2 "Named Insured," "You," "Your."

The "named insured" on a commercial business auto policy is often only the named business or corporation. Employees are usually covered only when they are occupying a covered business vehicle. This causes problems with small closely held corporations where the owner of the business often insures a "company car" in the company's name, but also drives the vehicle as their personal car. In *Haberman v The Hartford Ins. Group*, 443 F.3d 1257 (10th Cir., 2006), the named insured on a Hartford commercial policy was a professional corporation. However, Haberman, the owner of the corporation, was listed by name, in a "Named Persons Endorsement." The Endorsement said that it "modifies insurance provided under the...Business Auto Coverage Form" and that Haberman is an "'insured' for Liability Coverage" under the "Liability Coverage" section of the policy. Haberman was involved in an accident in a friend's vehicle and made a UM claim against the Hartford policy. Hartford argued that the Endorsement extended coverage to Haberman individually only under the Liability policy. However, the Tenth Circuit held that the language of the Endorsement plainly extended Haberman coverage under the entire Busienss Auto Coverage or, in the alternative, was at least ambiguous and could be read to extend coverage to Haberman to the entire Business Auto Coverage, which would include UM. This case is also discussed in §§1:2, 6:32, and 6:77.

§2:6 -Accident: Was it an intentional act or injury?

In *Equity Ins. v Garrett*, 2008 OK CIV APP 23, 178 P.3d 201, the insured was involved in a road rage incident. Her husband was outside the car fighting with the other driver and she used the car to bump the other driver to stop the fight. The Court of Civil Appeals held that, although the insured did not intend to injure the plaintiff, her actions were intentional and were likely to cause injury; thus, the injury was not an "accident" (and the intentional act exclusion also applied).

§2:7 -Accident: Was it an accident from the insured's point of view?

See *Farmers Alliance Mut. Ins. Co. v Salazar*, 77 F.3d 1291 (10th Cir. 1996), discussed in §2:9 below.

§2:9 -Occurrence: At what point in time, or at what place, does an "occurrence" occur? Including issues of negligent entrustment or negligent supervision. [New]

At what point in time does an "occurrence" occur? This can be important for such issues as determining whether an occurrence was within the coverage period. It can also be important in determining whether or not an "occurrence" has even occurred. This was the issue in *Farmers Alliance Mut. Ins. Co. v Salazar*, 77 F.3d 1291 (10th Cir. 1996). A homeowner's policy was issued to Ms. Salazar. Ms. Salazar gave a new silver pistol to her son Hector. Hector let his brother Manuel use the new pistol, and Manuel gave his old pistol to his friend, gang member, Jacob. Ms. Salazar knew that this had occurred. Manuel got involved in a gang altercation. Manuel and his companion fired bullets into a vehicle, and a bullet from his companion's gun struck and killed Thomas Byus. Manuel and Jacob were both convicted of first degree murder. Ms. Byus instituted a wrongful death action. The claim against Ms. Salazar was for "negligent supervision," and the claim against Manuel was for his "negligent entrustment" of the gun. The homeowner's insurer filed a declaratory judgment action. The District Court found that Ms. Salazar's actions qualified as an "occurrence," because she neither expected nor intended Byus' injury. However, the Court found that Manuel's actions were not an "occurrence," because Manuel expected and intended the injury.

The Tenth Circuit analyzed the case differently, at least as to Ms. Salazar's right to coverage. The Court said that it had to determine whether there was an "occurrence" as to Ms. Salazar. But, in order to do that, the Court first had to determine which event they would concentrate on. The two possible "events" were 1) Ms. Salazar giving the gun to Hector, and failing to stop Manuel (a known violent person) from taking it (the "negligent entrustment"), and 2) Manuel and Jacob getting into the subsequent gun battle which killed Byus. In finding coverage on Ms. Salazar's behalf, the

District Court had obviously concentrated on whether or not Ms. Salazar, at the time she negligently entrusted the gun, had expected or intended injury to Byus.

The Tenth Circuit first examined those cases where the time of the occurrence was in issue. The Tenth Circuit noted that, "The time of an "occurrence" most often becomes important in cases where the initial wrongdoing in a causal chain fell within the policy period but the resulting injury occurred after the expiration of the policy." *Id.* at 1295. The Court noted, in those types of cases, the date of the "occurrence" is usually held to be the date that the eventual damage took place, not the date of the original wrongful act.

The Court also examined those cases where the place of the occurrence was an issue. This is important when a policy limits coverage to occurrences within a certain geographical range, or to a certain place. The general rule in those situations is also that the "place" of the occurrence is determined by where the injury occurs, not where the wrongful act or negligence occurred.

Then the Court related this law to "negligent entrustment" by the following logic, *Id.* at 1296-7:

> ...We find that when determining whether a bodily injury was "caused by an occurrence" the question of whether there was an "occurrence" should be resolved by

> focusing on the injury and its immediately attendant causative circumstances. We reach this conclusion by means of simple deduction. If the time and place of an "occurrence" are determined by the time and place of the injury, then the acts which are said to constitute the "occurrence" must necessarily fall within the same temporal and spatial parameters. Looking at the facts of this case, we know that as a matter of firmly established law the supposed "occurrence" at issue in this case happened when and where [Jacob] murdered [Byus]. If we want to know which acts or omissions constituted this supposed "occurrence" we must focus our attention to the same time and place - to the murder itself. Though myriad other events of an earlier time and different place may have contributed to the claimed injury, to determine whether there was an "occurrence" within the meaning of the policy we must focus on those events directly responsible for the injury....

The Court went on to find that an "occurrence" must be an "accident;" that the murder was not an "accident," and that, therefore, the negligent supervision/entrustment claims against Ms. Salazar were not "occurrences" within the policy.

One wonders how this case would have been decided by the Oklahoma Supreme Court. The

Supreme Court is committed to the rule that whether an event is an "accident" is determined from the standpoint of the insured. See §2:7 in the main volume. Under the logic of its prior cases, even if it looked at the shooting as the operative "occurrence," the Supreme Court may have determined that, as to Ms. Salazar, the shooting was not an "accident."

§2:18 "Family Member" or "Relative"; "Resident of Household."

In *American Economy Ins. Co. v Bogdahn*, 2004 OK 9, 89 P.3d 1051, American's UM policy was issued to a family owned corporation (a pharmacy) as named insured. The pharmacist's child was injured while riding an uninsured all terrain vehicle. The question was whether the child was an "insured" under the pharmacy's UM policy. The UM policy defined "insured" as "If you are an individual, any 'family member.'" The term "family member" was defined as "a person related to you by blood, marriage or adoption who is a resident of your household, including a ward or foster child." The term "you" refers to "the Named Insured" (i.e.: the pharmacy). Obviously, since the pharmacy was not an "individual" (it was a corporation), it was incapable of having "family members." The Court held that this was not ambiguous, and that the child was not entitled to coverage under the pharmacy's UM policy.

§2:25 "Employee" and "Employer". [New]

In many commercial policies coverage questions can turn on the question of whether a certain person should be considered an "employee" of the named insured. In *Air Liquide America Corp. v Continental Cas. Co.,* 217 F.3d 1272 (10th Cir. 2002), the coverage question centered on whether the driver was an "employee," but, under the policy language, the term "employee" was left undefined. As a result, the Tenth Circuit held that the term was ambiguous. The Court held that an employment agency, who supplied a driver for a truck, could be held to be an "employer" of the driver for coverage purposes, even though the truck owner was the one who exercised day to day control over how the driver performed his duties.

§2:26 "Automobile," "Motor vehicle," "Private passenger car," "family car," "utility car."

In *Haworth v Jantzen*, 2006 OK 35, 172 P.3d 193, the insured had a farm and ranch policy that excluded coverage for "b. land motor vehicles subject to motor vehicle registration owned or operated or rented or loaned to an insured person." The insured was backing his pickup truck out of a driveway and caused an accident. The terms "land motor vehicle" and "land motor vehicle subject to registration" were not otherwise defined in the policy. In discussing the case, the Court noted that, in Oklahoma, the terms would be essentially synonymous because all "motor vehicles" are subject to registration in Oklahoma, and adding the word "land" to the front of the phrase, or the words "subject to registration" at the end, changed nothing. The pickup in question would be within the ambit of either phrase and the exclusion would apply.

However, the Court found that this exclusionary language, while unambiguous standing alone, created an ambiguity when read in conjunction with another exclusion that denied coverage for "c. land motor vehicles...if the bodily injury or property damage occurs away from the insured premises." The Court noted that exclusion "c." hinted that there might be coverage for "land motor vehicles" if the accident occurred when the pickup was not away from the insured premises. The perceived confusion created an ambiguity so that coverage was in order. "An insured could reasonably construe these provisions to mean that coverage of injury or damage arising out of the use of a land motor vehicle is: 1) always excluded; 2) only excluded if the vehicle is subject to registration; 3) only excluded if the injury occurs away from the insured premises; or 4) only excluded if the vehicle is not required to be registered and if the injury occurs away from the insured premises."

§2:42 - The Temporary Substitute Car.

The general purpose of the "temporary

substitute" provision was discussed at length in *Houston General Ins. Co. v American Fence Co.*, 115 F.3d 805 (10th Cir. 1997), discussed more fully in §2:43 below. In that opinion, the Tenth Circuit quoted, with approval, several outlines of the purpose of the "temporary substitute" provision, *Id.* at 807:

> The objective of the substitution provision is to afford temporary coverage to an insured who is using a borrowed vehicle because he or she is unable to use the vehicle designated in the policy for one of the specified reasons.... "[The] purpose is to provide 'continuous coverage' to insured while limiting risk to one operating vehicle at a time for a single premium."

§2:43 --The Requirement that the Described Car be Withdrawn from Normal Use Due to Breakdown.

In *Houston General Ins. Co. v American Fence Co.*, 115 F.3d 805 (10th Cir. 1997), the named insured was American Fence Co.. American Fence had just purchased a new 1992 pickup truck. The corporation had already added it onto its existing insurance policy as a described vehicle. The president of American Fence, John Woodie, and an American Fence employee, Jim Woodie, drove John's 1986 pickup to the dealership to pick up the new 1992 pickup. They planned that they would take the 1992 pickup to Cellular One to install a cellular telephone, and then drive home together in the 1986 pickup. John, the employee, drove Jim's 1986 pickup truck away from the dealership and headed towards Cellular One. However, on the way to Cellular One, John had an accident in Jim's pickup. Jim was still back at the dealership, picking up the new 1992 truck, when he received the call from John telling him about the accident.

Coverage for the accident was sought under the policy covering the 1992 pickup. The issue in the case was whether or not the 1992 pickup was temporarily out of service at the time of the accident so that the 1986 pickup could qualify as a temporary substitute for it. The Tenth Circuit refused coverage, holding that the 1992 pickup was not out of service at the time of the accident so that the 1986 pickup cold not qualify as a temporary substitute for it. The Court agreed that, under the *West* case discussed in the main volume, the 1992 pickup need not be totally disabled in order for coverage to apply. It is true that they were in the process of taking the 1992 pickup into Cellular One for what could qualify as "service" work. However, at the time of the accident, the 1992 pickup was completely serviceable and in Jim's possession. "Rather than being used in the place of the insured vehicle, the 1986 pickup was being used in addition to it for reasons of convenience." *Id.* at 808.

§2:47 -Non-Owned Cars.

§2:48 –In General.

For a case dealing with a rental vehicle as a "non-owned car," and how the Compulsory Liability Insurance Act affects coverage for a rental vehicle, see *Sisk v Gaines*, 2006 OK CIV APP 117, 144 P.3d 204, discussed at §2:52.

§2:52 Coverage for the insured's use of a rental car.

The practitioner needs to examine the policy language and determine whether there is an argument to be made, under the facts and policy language, that a rental vehicle may be either a "non-owned" vehicle or a "temporary substitute" vehicle. In either event, it often becomes important who the driver of such rental vehicles are because the owner of the vehicle (the rental agency) typically gives limited permission for their use only by the person signing the rental agreement and any additional authorized drivers.

If the question is whether the rental vehicle is covered by the terms of the renter's auto Liability policy, then the applicability of the Compulsory Liability Insurance Act, 47 O.S. §7-601, et. seq. (CLIA) needs to be considered. For example, see *Sisk v Gaines*, 2006 OK CIV APP 117, 144 P.3d 204. The Hudsons owned a vehicle insured by Allstate but it was in for repairs so the Hudsons rented a vehicle owned by Enterprise. Mr. Hudson had too much to drink, so he allowed Gaines to drive the rental car, with Mr. Hudson as a passenger, to get more beer. An accident ensued. The Oklahoma Court of Civil Appeals held that arguments about whether Gaines was a permissive user, and whether the rental vehicle was a non-owned or substitute vehicle under the Allstate policy were beside the point. Instead, the COCA simply held that the Allstate policy was compelled to provide Liability coverage to the rental vehicle (to the minimum required limits) because of the mandates of the CLIA.

Chapter 3: General Contract Provisions and Conditions.

§3:20 -Notice of Suit.

§3:21 --General.

If the insured breaches the obligation to give notice of suit, that breach may result in total loss of coverage. However, the Court has recognized that, in some circumstances, it may be more appropriate to simply reduce the coverage. This was discussed in *First Bank of Turley v Fidelity and Deposit Ins. Co. of Maryland*, 1996 OK 105, 928 P.2d 298, 308:

> The third question, as we understand

its meaning, asks whether the insured's failure to keep the insurer informed of critical post-denial developments affects the whole liability or goes solely to the issue of damages.

A tort-like comparison of the parties' degree of bad faith does not avail. Although the insured who fails to meet its duty-triggering conduct by giving deficient notice is not answerable ex delicto, the insured's inadequate notice avails to the insurer as a defense. If failure timely to provide critical information adversely affected the entire loss that was insured, it would avail as an absolute defense against liability (i.e., as in toto defense). That defense should show that the insured's failure to give adequate notice--not available from other sources--made it entirely impossible for the insurer to discharge its duty. On the other hand, if the defense were to be shown as having affected only an element (or portion) of the claimed loss, the defense could be invoked to defeat (pro tanto) that part of the total loss which was due to the insured's misperformance of its notice-giving duty.

These defenses depend on the impact of the insured's inadequate notice on the insurer's opportunity to meet its contractual obligation. We leave to the federal court the task of assessing the evidence to determine whether the insured's deficient performance of its duty-triggering conduct will avail here as a liability-defeating bar or merely as a pro tanto defense.

The *First Bank of Turley* case is discussed further in §3:23.

In *Baldridge v Kirkpatrick*, 2003 OK CIV APP 9, 63 P.3d 568, the Court of Civil Appeals held that the public policy behind the Compulsory Automobile Insurance Act required a liability insurer to provide coverage to a judgment even though the insurer admittedly never got notice of the lawsuit filed by the claimant against the insured. The "cooperation clause" of the policy had clearly been violated by the insured's failure to give notice of suit. However, the Court found that the public policy found in the Act required that the insurer provide coverage despite the failure to receive notice. But the Court refused to grant a complete victory to the claimant. The Court also held that it would violate concepts of due process for the insurer to be held liable for the judgment without having an opportunity to defend. Therefore, the Court remanded the case back to the trial court to allow the insurer to present a defense to the tort claim against its insured. This may seem like an empty victory for the third party claimant because he has to start over and retry his tort claim before he can obtain funds from the tortfesaor's insurer. However, without the "public policy" behind the Act, the claimant would not be able to collect against the Liability coverage at all because of the insured's violation of the cooperation clause. The result in the Baldridge case at least gives the claimant the chance to prove, anew, it's claim against the insured and establish a right of collection against the insurer.

§3:23 --The insured's obligation to advise the insurer of changed conditions, new information or amendments after original denial. [New]

An insured has an obligation to give the insurer notice of any suit filed against him. The insurer must then investigate and determine whether the facts would support whatever coverage claim is being made. If the insurer denies coverage, after the first notice of suit, is the insured obligated to keep the insurer up to date on later developments that may change the insurer's coverage opinion?

This question was discussed, in the context of a Liability policy, and the obligation to defend, in *First Bank of Turley v Fidelity and Deposit Ins. Co. of Maryland*, 1996 OK 105, 928 P.2d 298. The insured was sued for invasion of privacy, and turned the suit over to their Liability insurer to defend. The insured told the insurer that he had provided certain bank customer information to the IRS but that he was not sure whether this was legal or not ("he was uncertain as to what he was free to share with the authorities.") The insurer denied a defense on the grounds of "the insured's 'willful and intentional' violation of the Neeces' statutory privacy rights, which conduct brings the suit beyond the coverage provided by the policy."

However, in a subsequent "post-denial" deposition, the insured claimed that he was familiar with the privacy laws and that his actions fell within a statutory exception to them. This claim (that the insured was acting on his good-faith belief that his acts were not a willful violation of the privacy laws) was apparently never communicated to the insurer; nor was the insurer provided with a copy of this subsequent deposition. In later litigation between the insured Bank and the insurer, the insurer claimed that the Bank had an obligation to provide the insurer with notice of this newly acquired information (the deposition transcript) and that failure to provide it was "bad faith" on the insured's part. Once the insurer denied coverage, was the insured obligated to provide the insurer with new information that might impact on that decision?

The Court held that the insured had such an obligation, *Id* at 305:

> ...The insurer's liability for breach of its defense duty by refusal to provide a defense is measured by the facts that were known and

knowable--by what the insurer knows or by what the insurer was capable of discovering itself--at the time the insured's request was tendered.

As part of its notice-giving obligation, the insured must provide the insurer with facts material to its ascertainment of the duty to defend. A breach of the insured's obligation to give notice of critical post-denial developments may modify, excuse or defeat the insurer's performance under the contract. If the insured's performance of its contractual duty is deficient, the court must focus on whether (1) the initial notice was adequate to put the insurer on notice of potential liability under the policy, (2) the nondisclosed (or later-revealed) facts were so material that they should have been reported, (3) the notice was sufficient for the insurer's investigation and discovery of all the facts relative to its potential liability; and (4) the insurer's reasonable investigation could have uncovered the excluded information. None of these issues, if contested, can be resolved as a matter of law. Each is to be treated as a disputed fact for the trier.

§3:37 -Direct Actions by the Claimant Against the Insurer in a Liability Policy.

§3:38 –In General.

As noted in the Main Volume at footnote 79, statutes typically allowed the Liability insurer for motor carriers to be joined as party defendants in the lawsuit against their insured. However, recent federal and state statutory changes have made it more difficult to join such Liability insurers. In *Fierro v Lincoln General Ins. Co.*, 2009 OK CIV APP 62, 217 P.3d 158, the Court of Civil Appeals held that it was improper to join as party defendant the Liability carrier for an interstate motor carrier properly registered in its home state. The practitioner should closely examine the *Fierro* case for possible distinctions, such as whether the carrier is a certain type of intrastate motor carrier (who might be joined as a party). However, see *Mize v Liberty Mut. Ins. Co.*, 393 F.Supp.2d 1223 (W.D. OK. 2005) [statutory "motor carrier's" Liability insurer was a proper party defendant and jointly liable with defendant driver pursuant to 47 O.S. §230.30 (formerly 47 O.S. §169)].

§3:47 - The relationship between "primary," "excess" and "escape" clauses.

In *Oklahoma Farmers Union Mutual Insurance Company v. John Deere Insurance Company,* 1998 OK CIV APP 156, 967 P.2d 479 (discussed more fully in §4:45), the Court of Civil Appeals held that an "excess escape" clause was perfectly valid in an auto policy, as long as it left the insured with enough coverage, from other sources, to meet the minimum requirements of the Compulsory Liability Insurance Act.

American Cas. Co. of Reading, PA v Health Care Indem. Co., 520 F.3d 1131 (10th Cir., Ok., 2008) involved two professional liability insurance policies that provided coverage to the same insured. Both policies had clauses that provided that they only provided coverage if other insurance was exhausted first. The Tenth Circuit held that this essentially made both policies "excess" policies and the two carriers were obligated to share indemnity and defense cost obligations on a pro-rata basis.

§3:48 -What is other "similar insurance"?

"Self insurance" can, under certain circumstances, be "other insurance." In *Air Liquide America Corp. v Continental Cas. Co.*, 217 F.3d 1272 (10th Cir. 2002), the Tenth Circuit held that a $1 million "fronting policy" (a Liability policy where the insured's deductible is exactly equal to the policy limits) is actually a form of self-insurance. The insurer acts merely as a surety that the insured will pay any judgment covered under the policy. However, even though it is a form of "self-insurance," the "fronting policy" will still be considered "other collectible insurance" for purposes of an "excess" clause in an insurance policy. The Tenth Circuit held, at least in this situation, that "self insurance" is "other collectible insurance" when determining primary-excess status of insurers.

§3:68 The Liability/UM Coverage "set-off" (reduction of amounts owed by tortfeasor because of payments made by UM insurer). [New]

This section is about whether a Liability insurer (actually, a tortfeasor) can claim the right to reduce the amount it may owe because of an earlier payment by a UM insurer. Reduction of UM payments because of payments by a Liability insurer are discussed in §3:59 and §6:36.

In *Weatherly v Flournoy,* 1996 OK CIV APP 109, 929 P.2d 296, the claimant (representative of the deceased's estate) sought recovery against a UM insurer and a tortfeasor. He settled his claim against the UM insurer for $200,000, and the UM insurer waived its right of subrogation against the tortfeasor. The claimant continued his case against the tortfeasor and eventually got a judgment against the tortfeasor for $203,000. The tortfeasor argued that it should only owe $3,000, because the jury had set the damages at $203,000 and the claimant had already received $200,000. The Supreme Court disagreed, citing the "collateral source" rule. Under the collateral source rule, a tortfeasor is not entitled to claim credit for any amounts that a claimant might receive from other sources, unless it is from sources paid for by the tortfeasor. Here, the UM insurance payments were from a policy purchased by the claimant. Even though there may be some arguments that the claimant received "double recovery" in this case, the tortfeasor is in no position to complain, since she did not pay the UM premiums. The tortfeasor was required to suffer the entire judgment.

There are several things to notice here. First of all, this "set-off" is not really a contractual set-off provision. The "set-off" argued for by the tortfeasor (Liability insurer) in *Weatherly* is not found in the Liability policy; rather, it is an argument based on the perceived unfairness of a claimant receiving $403,000 in damages when a jury determined the damages to be $203,000. Since the argued-for "set-off" is not really based on policy language, it may be confusing to discuss it in the midst of other set-off provisions that are found in insurance policy language. However, if the reader were faced with a similar situation, this is the most logical portion of the book to look in.

Secondly, the reader should note that the *Weatherly* UM insurer waived its subrogation rights against the tortfeasor. If that had not occurred, the UM insurer would have likely sought return of its $200,000 payment out of the $203,000 judgment proceeds (if the tortfeasor had sufficient Liability insurance or assets to pay the judgment). This would have left the claimant with "only" $203,000 ($3,000 from the tortfeasor, and the original $200,000 UM payment). The Court held that the tortfeasor should not be heard to complain simply because the UM insurer chose to waive subrogation.

§3:76 -Anti-stacking provisions.

In *Nation v. State Farm Ins. Co.*, 1994 OK 54, 880 P.2d 877 there was some language that indicated that the Supreme Court may have approved of the "stacking" of Automobile Liability policies. However, this belief was put to rest in *Gordon v Gordon*, 2002 OK 5, 41 P.3d 391. Minor child was injured while a passenger in a vehicle driven by mother. Child sought the full $100,000 liability coverage available on the vehicle involved in the accident as well as stacking of the liability coverage on another household vehicle not involved in the accident. The Court reaffirmed the holding in *Nation*, that the "household exclusion" was against Oklahoma public policy, but that this only applied to amounts up to $10,000. The household exclusion could validly operate to exclude Liability coverage for amounts over $10,000. Further, the Court held that language in the "other insurance" and the "limits of liability" sections of the Liability policies validly prohibited stacking of the Liability policies.

§3:84 -Expiration of policy for Non-Payment.

In order to be an effective cancellation notice, the insurer's notice must do more than merely tell the insured that the policy "may" be cancelled if premiums are not paid. The notice must not be conditional. Rather, based on the policy language involved, the notice must advise the insured that cancellation has occurred because of non-payment and, obviously, such notice can not be given until the time for payment has passed. *Equity Ins. Co. v City of Jenks*, 2008 OK 27, 184 P.3d 541.

In *Poff v Oklahoma Farmers Union Mut. Ins. Co.*, 2006 OK CIV APP 3, 127 P.3d 646 the insurer sent an expiration notice to the insured advising him that his policy would expire unless the premium was paid by a date certain. The date passed, and a friend of the insured had an accident while driving the insured vehicle. The insured went to the agent's office and paid the premium, not telling the agent about the accident. The insurer issued a statement indicating that the policy was effective at 12:01 AM on the date the check was tendered to the insurer (i.e.: the insurer backdated coverage to the first minute of the date the check was tendered). Of course, the insurer was not aware that an accident had occurred prior to the time the check was tendered, yet after the "effective" time of the policy. Among other things, the insured argued that coverage was effective because the insurer waived timely payment of premium by backdating the coverage to several hours before the accident. The COCA acknowledged that, generally, an insurer will be held to the time of a backdated coverage. However, the COCA refused to hold the insurer to the backdated coverage in this case because the insurer was not aware of the intervening accident and "that one party cannot bind the other party to a contract of insurance through fraud or concealment." Id. at ¶18.

§3:86 -Notice of Cancellation. Mailing and Receipt of Notice.

Litigation involving an insurer's cancellation often involves proof of whether the insurer actually mailed out the cancellation notice. In *Kutz v State Farm Fire & Cas. Co.*, 2008 OK CIV APP 60, 189 P.3d 740 the Court held that the insurer upheld their burden of proof by showing that the notice made its way through their system. The insurer provided an affidavit that, after the notice was prepared, the insurer's normal business practice was to then place the notice in the mail.

§3:87 Severability clauses. [New]

Many policies contain "severability clauses" declaring that insureds will be treated separately under the policy. Here is the language of the severability provision in *BP America, Inc. v State Auto Prop. & Cas. Ins. Co.*, 2005 OK 65, 148 P.3d 832:

"Except with respect to the Limits of Insurance, and any rights or duties specifically assigned in this Coverage Part to the first Named Insured, this insurance applies:

a. As if each Named Insured were the only Named Insured; and

b. Separately as to each insured against whom claim is made or 'suit' is brought."

In general, the presence of a such a clause in a Liability policy will not create an ambiguity and should not be used to create coverage where none is intended. For a full discussion of the purpose and interpretation of severability clauses, see the *BP America* case at §17, et. seq.

Chapter 4: Liability Coverage.

§4:3 The validity of the contract. Fraud and misrepresentation. [New]

It is beyond the scope of this book to outline the complex rules that come into effect when it is discovered that an applicant may have lied during the application process. Lies during the application process can make the policy void or voidable under Oklahoma law, and an insurer can simply deny coverage, or bring an action for rescission to have the policy declared ineffective. For the law on this topic, generally, the reader is referred to 36 O.S. §3609, and the cases cited thereunder.

However, it is important to note that the rules for misrepresentation, fraud in the application, and the use of §3609, can change simply because the insurance policy in question happens to be an automobile Liability policy. In *Harkrider v Posey*, 2000 OK 94, 24 P.3d 821, the Supreme Court decided that a misrepresentation on an auto Liability insurance application, which might normally be sufficient to void coverage, could not be used to defeat payment to a third party claimant. The named insured had declared in the application that there was no other person in the household fourteen years of age or older. This was not true, as Raymond Posey, an unlicenced driver over the age of 14, was living in the household. Posey was driving the insured vehicle, with permission, and was involved in an accident. The Liability insurer claimed that, had it known of Posey's presence in the home, it would have issued the policy with a named-driver exclusion, excluding Posey from coverage. The insurer denied coverage because of the misrepresentation. Harkrider, the injured party, sued, obtained a judgment, and garnished the insurer's policy. The

Supreme Court first found that this type of misrepresentation caused the insurance policy to be "voidable" under 36 O.S. §3609; but the policy was not automatically "void" from the beginning. This was not "fraud in the execution" (fraud that misleads the party as to the true nature of the proposed agreement); rather, this was "fraud in the inducement," (fraud that misleads the party so as to create a false impression of the risks taken on by the insurer). Fraud in the execution leaves a contract "void ab initio" (from the beginning) while fraud in the inducement creates a valid contract that is merely voidable by the defrauded party. The distinction was important to the Court, because an innocent third party (such as Harkrider) can claim no rights under a "void" contract, but potentially could claim under a contract that was merely "voidable."

Had the policy been "void," it appears that the Court would have stopped its analysis at that point and ruled for the insurer. However, since a voidable contract is valid until declared void, the Court had to decide whether the insurer could defeat the rights of the innocent claimant. The Court noted that insurers, under traditional Liability policies that were not statutorily mandated, could potentially defeat a claimant's rights under a "voidable" policy. However, the Court held that the public policy of protecting the public from the negligence of operators of motor vehicles, expressed in the Compulsory Automobile Liability Insurance Act (CALIA), 47 O.S. §7-600, et.

seq., was more important than the insurer's right to protect itself from a voidable policy. The Court noted that insurers can protect themselves through adequate investigation of application answers before issuing a policy. The Court also noted that the policy in suit did not exceed the $10,000 limits mandated by the CALIA; thus the Court did not need to decide whether the policy would be void for amounts past the $10,000 statutory limit.

§4:5 The insuring clause.

§4:7 -"Damages" or "All sums." Insurer's liability for punitive damages.

The duty to settle a case in good faith, the duty to settle when "covered" and "uncovered" damages are mixed in the same claim, and the duty to settle when the insured has been sued for punitive damages, were discussed in *Magnum Foods, Inc. v Continental Cas. Co.*, 36 F.3d 1491 (10th Cir. 1994). See §4:62 below.

§4:11 – "Arising out of."

Federal Ins. Co. v Tri-State Ins. Co., 157 F.3d 800 (10th Cir.1998) was a declaratory judgment action brought by a General Liability insurer to recover indemnification from another insurer who had issued a Business Auto Policy. An explosion occurred when the operator of a truck stopped to pump material from a storage tank. The truck's engines were running and fumes caused the explosion which burned the truck operators. One of the issues was whether the "Operations Exclusion" in the Business Auto Policy would apply. This clause denied coverage if the bodily injury was "arising out of the operation of" certain equipment that was listed in the policy. One of the banned pieces of equipment was a "pump." The Court of Appeals noted that the fire was caused when a vacuum pump on the truck pulled fumes out of the tank and the fumes were ignited by the engine. Under those facts, did the injury "arise out of" the use of the pump? If it did, there would be no coverage.

The Court said that Oklahoma did not require that an item be the actual "proximate cause" of an injury before that injury could be said to "arise out of" the use of the item. Rather, Oklahoma has adopted a "chain of events" test. Since the vacuum pump was in the "chain of events" that led up to the explosion and injury, the Court held that the Operations Exclusion applied, and the Business Auto Policy had no coverage.

The Court also said that "the general consensus [is] that the phrase 'arising out of' should be given a broad reading such as 'originating from' or 'growing out of' or ''flowing from' or 'done in connection with' – that is, it requires some causal connection to the injuries suffered, but does not require proximate cause in the legal sense." *Id.* at

804.

Further, the Court declined to interpret the phrase more narrowly just because it was found in language of exclusion rather than language of inclusion. *Id.* at 804-05. For discussion of this general "rule of construction" see §1.2.

§4.12 – "Use" of a Motor Vehicle.

In *State, ex rel.Crawford v Indemnity Underwriters Insurance Company*, 1997 OK CIV APP 38, 943 P.2d 1102, the accident occurred when the insured pickup truck was used to illuminate a stalled trailer that was carrying a backhoe. The backhoe's bucket swung around and hit an oncoming vehicle. The question was whether or not the accident could be said to be caused by the "use" of the insured pickup truck. The Court of Civil Appeals held that the use of the pickup was not the cause of the accident, citing the "chain of events" test.

§4:34 -Use within the Scope of Consent of the Named Insured. Permissive Use. The Omnibus Clause.

§4:35 –The Omnibus Clause, In General.

In *O'Neill v Long*, 2002 OK 63, 54 P.3d 109, the Supreme Court changed the rules in Oklahoma regarding "permission" and the "second permittee."

The Supreme Court held that, under the Compulsory Liability Insurance Act, an "omnibus clause" in Oklahoma must extend coverage to all persons driving the vehicle with the permission of the named insured, whether or not the use being made of the vehicle at the time of the accident exceeds the scope of the permission granted. In the *O'Neill* case, the permittee exceeded the scope of his permission because he allowed another driver to use the vehicle despite the fact that the owner expressly told the permittee not to allow the car to be driven by anyone else. The Court held that the use by the third party (the "second permittee") was a use beyond the scope of the permission granted by the named insured. However, the insurer had to provide coverage for this use of the vehicle because the Compulsory Liability Insurance Act required it. Thus, the *O'Neill* case must now be considered when dealing with cases involving "scope of permission" and cases involving the "second permittee" rule. Like the other decisions dealing with the application of the Compulsory Liability Insurance Act, the Court held that it only applied to the minimum required coverage under the Act ($10,000/20,000). As to amounts of coverage exceeding the minimum limits, the law remains unchanged and the terms of the contract control.

§4:36 –Express Permission under the Omnibus Clause. "Second Permittee" Rules.

The Supreme Court's decision in *O'Neill v Long*, 2002 OK 63, 54 P.3d 109 changes the analysis of the "second permittee" situation, at least up to the $10,000 minimum limits required under the Compulsory Liability Insurance Act. See the discussion in §4:35 above.

§4:45 - Non-traditional definitions of "insured."

Oklahoma Farmers Union Mutual Insurance Company v. John Deere Insurance Company, 1998 OK CIV APP 156, 967 P.2d 479. Jerry Hausman delivered a car to Hudiburg Chevrolet, Inc., a Midwest City auto dealership and garage, for service. The car was owned by his mother, Dollie Hausman. Hudiburg loaned Jerry another vehicle to drive while his mother's car was being serviced. While driving the loaner, Jerry had an accident, injuring a passenger. The passenger made claim against Liability and UM policies covering Jerry and Dollie's personal vehicles (OFU) and against John Deere, whose policy covered Hudiburg. OFU and Hudiburg settled with the claimant, and presented the ultimate question of which insurer was liable for the loss to the Court.

The Court of Civil Appeals noted that John Deere's policy which excluded any of Hudiburg's "customers, if your business is shown in the Declarations as an "auto" dealership." However, if the "customer" had no other insurance, then the customer would be covered up to the compulsory liability insurance limits. John Deere characterized Jerry as a "customer" of Hudiburg; however OFU argued that Jerry was not a customer of the "dealership" aspect of Hudiburg's business, but only of the "repair shop" aspect.

The Court held that it was sufficient that Jerry was a "customer" of Hudiburg's garage business, and that OFU's policy provided sufficient coverage to meet the minimum requirements of the Compulsory Liability Insurance law in Oklahoma. Therefore, under the terms of John Deere's policy, Jerry was not covered for Liability coverage while driving the loaned vehicle. Coverage would only be provided by OFU.

In many commercial policies coverage questions can turn on the question of whether a certain person should be considered an "employee" of the named insured. In *Air Liquide America Corp. v Continental Cas. Co.,* 217 F.3d 1272 (10th Cir. 2002), the coverage question centered on whether the driver was an "employee," but, under the policy language, the term "employee" was left undefined. As a result, the Tenth Circuit held that the term was ambiguous. The Court held that an employment agency, who supplied a driver for a truck, could be held to be an "employer" of the driver for coverage purposes, even though the truck owner was the one who exercised day to day control over how the driver performed his duties.

Continental's policy provided coverage to "employees...while using a covered auto you don't own...in your business." The Court held that it would cover the employee of an employment agency, even though the agency had contracted the employee's services to drive trucks for another company. The employee was driving a truck for the other company at the time of the accident; but he was still driving the truck in the employment agency's "business" because the agency was in the business of providing employees to its clients.

American Economy Ins. Co. v Bogdahn, 2004 OK 9, 89 P.3d 1051 is a UM case, but is helpful in interpreting commercial policies that sometimes use such terms as "family member." American's UM policy was issued to a family owned corporation (a pharmacy) as named insured. The pharmacist's child was injured while riding an uninsured all terrain vehicle. The question was whether the child was an "insured" under the pharmacy's UM policy. The UM policy defined "insured" as "If you are an individual, any 'family member.'" The term "family member" was defined as "a person related to you by blood, marriage or adoption who is a resident of your household, including a ward or foster child." The term "you" refers to "the Named Insured" (i.e.: the pharmacy). Obviously, since the pharmacy was not an "individual" (it was a corporation), it was incapable of having "family members." The Court held that this was not ambiguous, and that the child was not entitled to coverage under the pharmacy's UM policy.

§4:60 The Duty to Defend.

§4:61 -In General.

First Bank of Turley v Fidelity and Deposit Ins. Co. of Maryland, 1996 OK 105, 928 P.2d 298 is a case involving the duty to defend. It contains an extensive discussion of the obligation to defend, how it is determined, reservation of rights and the results of a refusal to defend. This case may be used as a good general overview of the duty to defend. However, the primary issue in the case is how to treat a situation where the insured failed to give an insurer notice of changes in the nature of the claim asserted against the insured. The obligation of the insured to give notice of the claim, and the *Bank of Turley* case is discussed in detail at §3:21. However, we quote here the Court's general discussion of the duty to defend, *Bank of Turley* at 304-5:

> ...The relationship between the insured and insurer is contractual in nature. An insurer's duty to defend claims against its insured is an ex contractu obligation. A liability insurance policy generally contains two basic duties--the duty to defend and the duty to indemnify its insured. The insurer's

primary duty is to provide indemnity for loss or to pay a specified amount upon determinable contingencies. The duty to defend is separate from, and broader than, the duty to indemnify, but the insurer's obligation is not unlimited. The defense duty is measured by the nature and kinds of risks covered by the policy as well as by the reasonable expectations of the insured. An insurer has a duty to defend an insured whenever it ascertains the presence of facts that give rise to the potential of liability under the policy. The insurer's defense duty is determined on the basis of information gleaned from the petition (and other pleadings), from the insured and from other sources available to the insurer at the time the defense is demanded (or tendered) rather than by the outcome of the third-party action.

An insurer ordinarily has no duty to defend an insured absent a request to provide a defense, which act serves to trigger the insurer's performance under the contract. It is the insured's sole duty to give its insurer timely and adequate notice of a third-party claim to aid the insurer in the discovery of facts bearing on coverage. Once an insurer receives notice of a claim and proof of loss, the insurer should evaluate the matter and make a reasonable investigation to determine whether a potential for coverage exists. An insured in turn has an obligation to cooperate with the insurer, which is both contractual and implied in law. An insurer who disputes the insured's demand to defend has three options. It can (1) seek declaratory relief that would define the insurer's rights and obligations; (2) defend the insured under a reservation of rights, or (3) refuse to take any action at the peril of being later found in breach of its duty to defend.

The insurer's liability for breach of its defense duty by refusal to provide a defense is measured by the facts that were known and knowable--by what the insurer knows or by what the insurer was capable of discovering itself--at the time the insured's request was tendered.

In *Air Liquide America Corp. v Continental Cas. Co.*, 217 F.3d 1272 (10th Cir. 2002). The Tenth Circuit held that an insurer may, by appropriate language in its policy, disclaim any duty to defend its insured, even for covered losses. If the primary insurer effectively disclaims, through appropriate policy language, any duty to defend its insured, then the duty to defend would fall to any excess carrier who does have a contractual duty to defend.

§4:62 -Control of the Defense and Settlement.

§4:62

The case of *Magnum Foods, Inc. v Continental Cas. Co.*, 36 F.3d 1491 (10th Cir. 1994) also contains a good general discussion of the obligation to defend from the Tenth Circuit's perspective. The Court notes that once the obligation to defend is undertaken, the insurer must "meet a high standard of conduct.... The right to control the litigation carries with it certain duties... One of those is the duty not to prejudice the insured's rights by failing to request special interrogatories or a special verdict in order to clarify coverage of damages.... " *Id.* at 1498. Because of the insurer's ability to seek clarification of the types of damages being awarded at trial, "If it were impossible to determine on what basis the jury made its award, the damages would presumed to be covered." *Id.* at 1499. The Court conducted an extensive review of the jury instructions in order to determine on what basis the jury award was rendered so that it could be determined whether the verdict was a covered loss. Further, "the duty to defend is distinct from and broader than, the duty to indemnify.... When an insurer owes or undertakes the duty to defend its insured in a suit seeking both insured and uninsurable damages, it has the duty to conduct settlement negotiations in good faith as part of that defense. For one thing, this includes warning the insured of any potential exposure to him and appraising him of settlement opportunities within a reasonable time after they are presented." *Id.* at 1506.

We believe that where, as here, there is a substantial risk of a large verdict for which the insured will be held liable, an insurer may not refuse to cooperate with its insured in settling the claims merely because the insurer has an honest belief in its ability to defend the insured. As a professional in the defense of such cases, the insurer who undertakes the defense of its insured must use a degree of skill commensurate with such professional standards... The insurer must exercise "diligence, intelligence, good faith, honest and conscientious fidelity to the common interest of the parties."...The parties have a common interest in settling the law suit if they can do so for less than it would cost them if the case went to trial. Even in situations where the insurer will only have to indemnify the insured for a portion of the judgment rendered against it, good faith requires that neither party act in such a way as to deprive the other of the benefits of the agreement... If an insurer fails to act cooperatively to reach a settlement - for example, by refusing to make a reasonable offer to settle at least the insured portion of the claim - then the insurer's conduct may be reasonably perceived as tortious, and the trial court may submit the issue of bad faith to the jury...

Id. at 1508.

The *Magnum Foods* case also dealt with the issue of how an insurer must handle the defense of a claim that includes uninsurable punitive damages along with insurable damages. Under Oklahoma law, punitive damages are generally uninsurable (see the discussion in §4:7 in the main volume). An insurer has a duty to handle claims against an insured in good faith and to settle them within policy limits when reasonably possible (see the discussion in §4:81 in the main volume). The *Magnum Foods* case discussed the tension between the insurer's obligation to settle cases within policy limits, and the law's desire that the insurer not be required to pay for an insured's punitive damage exposure. The entire discussion is too extensive for this work; however, in general, the insurer is not required to settle a covered claim just to insulate an insured from a punitive damage claim, but the insurer must also work cooperatively with the insured to settle the case and avoid the punitive damage exposure. See *Magnum Foods* at 1502-6.

§4:65 -Duty Determined by the Allegations of the Petition or by the Facts Discoverable Through a Reasonable Investigation.

The effect of exclusions held invalid under the Compulsory Liability Insurance Act.

The duty to defend is closely aligned with questions of "coverage." If an insurer has a duty to indemnify an insured under the language of the policy then it is a good general rule, absent any other issues, that the insurer will also have a duty to defend that insured. However, what happens if the insurance policy clearly does not provide Liability coverage by its terms (because of an exclusion), but that exclusion is held invalid under the Compulsory Liability Insurance Act? This question is discussed in §4:68.

§4:68 The effect of exclusions held invalid under the Compulsory Liability Insurance Act. [New]

The duty to defend is closely aligned with questions of "coverage." If an insurer has a duty to indemnify an insured under the language of the policy then it is a good general rule, absent any other issues, that the insurer will also have a duty to defend that insured. However, what happens if the insurance policy clearly does not provide Liability coverage by its terms (because of an exclusion), but that exclusion is held invalid under the Compulsory Liability Insurance Act?

This question was discussed in *Ball v Wilshire Ins. Co.*, 2009 OK 38, 221 P.3d 717. A garage owner loaned a vehicle to a customer while the customer's car was being repaired. The vehicle was insured under a garage policy issued to the garage owner.

The policy had an a "Loaned Vehicle" exclusion that would deny coverage if the vehicle were loaned to customers (such as when the customer's car was being repaired). Wilshire denied Liability and UM coverage on the vehicle after it was involved in an accident while being driven by a customer. The Court held that the exclusion was invalid under the Compulsory Liability Insurance Act (CLIA), which meant that the insurer would have to provide at least the minimum statutory coverage for the vehicle.

However, the Court also held that just because the CLIA required the insurer to provide minimum amounts of indemnity to permissive users of the vehicle did not mean that the CLIA required the insurer to provide a defense under the policy. The obligation to indemnify and the obligation to defend are two different things and the CLIA only expressed a public policy that vehicles have certain monetary levels of insurance coverage available; the statute said nothing about requiring the insurer to defend the insured.

The Court had often held that the CLIA did not require insurers to provide coverage that was outside the mandates of the CLIA. For example, if an insurance policy has \$100,000/\$300,000 limits of liability, but has an exclusion denying coverage under certain circumstances, then that exclusion may be found invalid under the CLIA. If it is found invalid, however, the insurer's obligation to pay is not measured by the \$100,000 policy limits but by the minimum amount of coverage required by the CLIA. The result would be the insurer would, under current law, be required to provide $25,000/$50,000 in coverage. In Ball the Court extended that logic to the obligation to defend: since the CLIA said nothing about the duty to defend, if an exclusion is held invalid under the CLIA it does not mean that the insurer has a duty to defend.

> ¶18 Our Compulsory Liability Insurance Law mandates that vehicles be secured against liability to innocent victims where harm occurs from a vehicle's negligent operation. It does not mandate an insurer-provided defense of persons driving vehicles that are secured by operation of the Compulsory Liability Insurance Law. The statutory omnibus clause displaces only those insurance policy provisions that are incompatible with the law's intent to provide minimal compensation to an injured third party. The person whose minimal coverage is law-mandated is not entitled to the insurer's performance of purely contractual obligations that stand outside the law's mandate. This rule gives effect to the public policy underlying the Compulsory Liability Insurance Law while refraining from unduly interfering with the parties' freedom to contract, which can be restricted only in the name of articulated public policy.

However, the Court was concerned that insurers would use this decision as a mandate to avoid defense obligations. The Court issued an unusual warning to insurers:

> ¶19 Oklahoma's decisional law is by now firmly established that liability exclusions, no matter the identity of the class of persons excluded, which diminish the protection afforded by the Compulsory Liability Insurance Law will not be enforced as to minimal statutory liability coverage, except as permitted by existing law. Today's pronouncement, recognizing that the duty to defend is not a part of the Law's mandate, should not be taken by the insurance industry as a license to place or leave in place unenforceable exclusions in policies in a manner that misleads insureds as to the insurer's other, dependent contractual obligations. Should flagrant and persistent abuses arise, the court might find itself impelled to reconsider the point addressed by today's decision. It would be advantageous for all concerned if insurers would draft their policies to take into account today's pronouncement.

Determining the meaning and intent of this paragraph will likely require further litigation and court decisions. The Court left another question unstated: if an insurer is "forced" into indemnity obligations because of the CLIA, but has no defense obligations under the terms of the contract Ball), can the insurer still require the insured to allow the insurer to take over and contol the defense, and does the insured have to cooperate in that defense under the terms of the contract?

§4:70 -The Obligation of One Insurer to Contribute to Another for the Cost of Defending their Joint Insured.

Also see *USF&G v Federated Rural Elec. Ins. Corp.*, 2001 OK 81, 37 P.3d 828, where the Court held that an excess Liability insurer is not obligated to reimburse any of the costs of defense expended by the primary Liability policy, at least until the primary policy is exhausted. This is true even if the claim against the insured, if paid, would exceed the amount of the primary policy. This case includes a discussion of the differences between contribution and equitable subrogation. Obviously this case leaves open the possibility that, once the primary policy is exhausted by payment, if the primary policy expends any further amounts for defense, then the excess policy may be required to reimburse.

§4:75 -The Obligation to Pay for Independent Counsel in a Conflict of Interest.

In *Nisson v. American Home Assurance Co.*, 1996 OK CIV APP 40, 917 P.2d 488, the Liability insurer stood ready to provide a defense to its insured. However, the insurer was providing a defense under a reservation of rights because of a coverage question (the coverage of sexual acts under a psychologist's professional liability policy). They were also providing a defense to the psychologist's business partners. Insurance defense counsel, who represented both groups of defendants, wanted to pursue a line of defense for the partners that would present a conflict of interest between the partners and the psychologist. Nisson sought private counsel, and the private counsel made demand on the insurer to allow them to represent Nisson, at the insurer's expense. Insurer refused.

The Court of Civil Appeals noted that there were competiting equities. The insured should not be able to cry "conflict" anytime it wants to and force the insurer to hire private counsel. The insurer should not be able to force the insured into accepting defense counsel who are genuinely in a conflict and who would present a half-hearted defense. The Court discussed cases on both sides of this equation, and made these comments:

> ...not every perceived or potential conflict of interest automatically gives rise to a duty on the part of the insurer to pay for the insured's choice of independent counsel....That is:

> Independent counsel is only necessary in cases where the defense attorney's duty to the insured would require that he defeat liability on any ground and his duty to the insurer would require that he defeat liability only upon grounds that would render the insurer liable.... Conversely, absent a threat of divided loyalty between the insured and insurer, no need for retention of independent counsel arises because the issue of coverage is then separate from the issue of liability.

Under the facts of this case, where a real conflict of interest existed between the two sets of defendants being represented by the same insurance defense counsel, the Court held that the insurer should pay a reasonable amount of attorneys fees for insured's private counsel to resolve the conflict.

§4:80 The Duty to Settle

§4:81 -In General.

The duty to settle a case in good faith, the duty to settle when "covered" and "uncovered" damages are mixed in the same claim, and the duty to settle when the insured has been sued for punitive damages, were discussed in *Magnum Foods, Inc. v Continental Cas. Co.*, 36 F.3d 1491 (10th Cir. 1994). See §4:62 above.

§4:81

Although the subject of bad faith is outside the scope of this book, the insurer's "duty to settle" is entwined with its duty to pay and right to control the defense of the suit. Thus, some citation to bad faith cases is in order. Most significant in this regard is *Badillo v Mid Century Ins. Co.*, 2005 OK 48, 121 P.3d 1080. The insured was involved in an accident and the Liability insurer was on the verge of paying its $10,000 policy limit to settle the claim. The insurer tendered its full policy limit to settle the claim, but the claimant refused to accept until claimant was allowed to take a statement from the insured. Claimants were suspicious that the insured had been intoxicated and that he may have been in the course of his employment at the time of the accident. The Liability insurer refused to allow claimants to take the statement because it was allegedly concerned about his client's potential criminal liability. The insurer did not discuss this decision with the insured. Settlement negotiations broke down and claimants went on to obtain a $600,000 verdict against the insured. The Court's final opinion included a detailed discussion of bad faith law and a Liability insurer's obligation to its insured. Again, the details of that discussion are beyond the scope of this work; however counsel for insurer and insured should be well aware of this discussion because the question of bad/good faith often overshadow legal and tactical decisions in this area of law. Also see *Milroy v Allstate Ins. Co.*, 2007 OK CIV APP 6, 151 P.3d 922.

§4:88 - Prejudgment Interest.

As stated in the text, some insurers make themselves liable for prejudgment interest, over and above the policy limits. This occurred in *Federal Ins. Co. v Tri-State Ins. Co.*, 157 F.3d 800 (10th Cir. Okla 1998), where the insurance policy said:

> We will pay, with respect to any "claim" or "suit" we defend: ...6. Prejudgment interest awarded against the insured on that part of the judgment we pay. If we make an offer to pay the applicable limit of insurance, we will not pay any prejudgment interest based on that period of time after the offer.. . . . .These payments will not reduce the limits of insurance.

Based on this language, the Court required the insurer to pay the insured's prejudgment interest exposure under the Liability policy, even though the policy limits were otherwise exhausted.

Sometimes a Liability insurer can become liable for prejudgment interest, above their policy limits, even if the policy language does not require it. In *McDonald v Schreiner*, 2001 OK 58, 28 P.3d 574, a medical malpractice insurer's policy provided for certain policy limits, and also promised to pay "claims expenses" defined as "fees, costs and expenses which result from the investigation, adjustment, defense and appeal of a claim." The insurer chose to defend the case. rather than to settle and pay the claim. The Court held that the prejudgment interest that accrued while the insurer decided to defend, rather than negotiate and pay, a claim, was an expense that arose because of the strategic choices made by the insurer during the defense of the claim. Under those facts, the prejudgment interest was a "claims expense" under the wording of the policy, and the insurer was liable for it without regard to the policy limits.

However, different facts caused a different result in *Parish v Henry*, 2004 OK 62, 97 P.3d 646. In that case it was the insured physician who had refused to give his consent for settlement of the case within policy limits. Under the terms of the malpractice policy, all settlements had to be with the written consent of the insured. The insured withheld consent, and the case went to judgment. The Court held that, under those facts, it was the insured who had delayed payment and settlement, not the insurer. Thus, it was not unfair to place the financial burden for the delay, represented by the prejudgment interest award, on the insured rather than the insurer.

The applicability of the *Parish* decision may be limited. We note that very few Liability insurance policies contain the "insured's consent to settle" provision that was critical to the *Parish* case.

However, *Parish* may result in post-judgment litigation where the insured and the insurer argue about whose conduct (insurer or insured) actually caused the case not to settle at an earlier date.

§4:95 Compulsory Liability Insurance, Financial Responsibility and Out of State Coverage.

§4:97 -The effect of the Financial Responsibility Laws, including the Compulsory Liability Insurance Act, on the interpretation of insurance policies.

For a case dealing with a rental vehicle as a "non-owned car," and how the Compulsory Liability Insurance Act affects coverage for a rental vehicle, see *Sisk v Gaines*, 2006 OK CIV APP 117, 144 P.3d 204, discussed at §2:52.

§4:99 –The effect of the CLIA on policy interpretation.

In *Baldridge v Kirkpatrick*, 2003 OK CIV APP 9, 63 P.3d 568, the Court of Civil Appeals held that the public policy behind the Compulsory Automobile Insurance Act required a liability insurer to provide coverage to a judgment even though the insurer admittedly never got notice of the lawsuit filed by the claimant against the insured. The "cooperation clause" of the policy had clearly been violated by the insured's failure to give notice of suit. However, the Court found that the public policy found in the Act required that the insurer provide coverage despite the failure to receive notice. But the Court refused to grant a complete victory to the claimant. The Court also held that it would violate concepts of due process for the insurer to be held liable for the judgment without having an opportunity to defend. Therefore, the Court remanded the case back to the trial court to allow the insurer to present a defense to the tort claim against its insured. This may seem like an empty victory for the third party claimant because he has to start over and retry his tort claim before he can obtain funds from the tortfesaor's insurer. However, without the "public policy" behind the Act, the claimant would be left with a completely uncollectible judgment, because of the insured's violation of the cooperation clause. The result in the Baldridge case at least gives the claimant the chance to prove, anew, it's claim against the insured and establish a right of collection against the insurer.

Other cases involving the effect of the CLIA have been decided:

- *O'Neill v Long*, 2002 OK 63, 54 P.3d 109 [rules regarding "permissive use" and the "omnibus clause."] See §§4:35, 4:36.

- *Oklahoma Farmers Union Mutual Insurance Company v. John Deere Insurance Company,* 1998 OK CIV APP 156, 967 P.2d 479 [the validity of "excess escape" clauses]. See §§3:47, 4:45.

- *Harkrider v Posey*, 2000 OK 94, 24 P.3d 821 [whether an Auto Liability policy can be voided for fraud in the application.] See §4:3.

§4:103 The Plaintiff's failure to comply with the Compulsory Insurance Law. [New]

In an apparent attempt to encourage Oklahoma drivers to keep minimum amounts of Liability Insurance on their vehicles, the Oklahoma Legislature has enacted 47 O.S. § 7-116 which limits the amount of damages a Plaintiff can recover if that Plaintiff does not have the required Compulsory Liability Insurance at the time of the accident. Note, this is a tort damage limitation and the emphasis of this book is on insurance coverage issues. However, to aid the practitioner, we provide the full text of the statute here. The statute is effective November 1, 2011.

47 O.S. § 7-116

> A. Except as provided in subsection B of this section, in any civil action to recover damages arising out of an accident involving the operation of a motor vehicle or for any claim against the motor vehicle liability insurance coverage of another party, the maximum amount that a plaintiff or claimant may receive, if the plaintiff or claimant is not in compliance with the Compulsory Insurance

Law, shall be limited to the amount of medical costs, property damage, and lost income and shall not include any award for pain and suffering.

B. The limitations provided for in subsection A of this section shall not apply:

1. If the plaintiff or claimant was injured by a motorist who at the time of the accident was operating or using a motor vehicle while under the influence of drugs or alcohol in violation of any provision of law relating to the illegal operation or use of a motor vehicle while under the influence of drugs or alcohol, and that motorist:

a. was convicted of, or pled guilty or nolo contendere to, the offense, or

b. dies as a result of the accident if it is proven by a preponderance of the evidence that the motorist was operating or using the motor vehicle while under the influence of drugs or alcohol in violation of any provision of law relating to the illegal operation or use of a motor vehicle while under the influence of drugs or alcohol;

2. If the plaintiff or claimant was a passenger in a motor vehicle involved in the accident, unless the plaintiff or claimant is an owner of the vehicle;

3. If the plaintiff or claimant was not in any motor vehicle involved in the accident;

4. To wrongful death claims;

5. If the motorist who caused the accident:

   a. intentionally caused the accident,

   b. left the scene of the accident, or

   c. at the time of the accident, was acting in furtherance of the commission of a felony;

6. If, at the time of the accident, the plaintiff or claimant was claimed as a dependent on the federal income tax

return of one or both parents of the plaintiff or claimant and the parent or parents were not in compliance with the Compulsory Insurance Law; or

7. If, at the time of the accident, the plaintiff or claimant previously had been covered by an insurance policy meeting the requirements of the Compulsory Insurance Law that was terminated or nonrenewed for failure to pay the premium, unless at least thirty (30) days prior to the accident notice of termination was sent to the last-known mailing address of the policyholder.

C. Each person who is involved in the accident which is the basis for the action or claim by the plaintiff or claimant and who is found liable for damages to the plaintiff or claimant may assert the limitation of recovery provided for in subsection A of this section, unless the provisions of subsection B of this section apply. The motor vehicle liability insurer of the person asserting the limitation of recovery also may assert the limitation.

Exclusion.

<u>Hartline v Hartline</u>

In *Hartline v Hartline*, 2001 OK 15, 39 P.3d 765, the Supreme Court reexamined the household exclusion and somewhat modified the test for determining its validity (and the validity of other Liability policy exclusions). Wife was a passenger in a car with the Husband driving. There was an accident caused by Husband's negligence. Wife filed suit against Husband, and judgment was taken. Wife then garnished Husband's Mid Century Liability policy, upon which Husband was the only "named insured" reflected on the declarations page. Husband had rejected UM coverage, and there were no other vehicles in the household, so the only funds available to pay the judgment was the Husband's liability policy. However, the Liability policy had an "insured person" exclusion that denied coverage "for bodily injury to an insured person." "Insured person" was defined in the policy as 1) the named insured, 2) the named insured's spouse, and 3) relatives of either, living in the household. Wife would be excluded from coverage because she was the named insured's spouse and because she was a "relative" of the named insured.

***<u>Looney</u>* <u>reversed</u>.**

The trial court ruled against Mid Century and

the Court of Civil Appeals reversed. The argument turned on an analysis of two of the Supreme Court's previous cases. First, the Court examined *Looney v Farmers Insurance Group*, 1980 OK 111, 616 P.2d 1138, and ended up overruling it. *Looney* had held that, under similar facts, Oklahoma's compulsory automobile liability insurance laws did not invalidate a "household" exclusion. The *Hartline* Court made several points in overruling *Looney*:

> That *Looney* was decided soon after the advent of the Compulsory Automobile Liability Insurance Act (CALIA), and the Courts had not yet fully developed the "public policy" underlying the Act that required that injured members of the public be protected from injury from automobiles;
>
> That the *Looney* opinion had made reference to permissible exclusions found in another Article of Title 47, rather than the Article containing the CALIA;
>
> That the CALIA had been amended since the *Looney* decision.

<u>*Nation* modified to require an examination of other available coverages.</u>

Further, the Court examined the more recent case of *Nation v State Farm Insurance Company*,

1994 OK 54, 880 P.2d 877, where the Court had held that State Farm could not validly withhold payment for injuries suffered by the named insured's five year old son based on State Farm's household exclusion. *Nation* had held that, under the CALIA, the exclusion was invalid, at least as to the first $10,000 in coverage. The Court did not overrule *Nation*, but noted that the *Nation* decision only invalidated "the exclusionary clause there in contest without providing any gauge for determining invalidity in future cases." Id. at ¶12, 39 P.3d 770. The Court seemed to say that the *Nation* exclusion and the *Hartline* exclusions were different and that the *Hartline* exclusion was "overbroad" in that it merged the "named insured" and the "household" exclusions into a single "insured exclusion" clause. The Court did not otherwise explain why the *Nation* exclusion and the *Hartline* exclusion were functionally different, or why this made a difference to their analysis.

The Court re-examined the CALIA and noted that it had been amended to allow for "exclusions in accordance with existing law." Although this language would seem to allow certain common exclusions (such as the "insured exclusion"), the Court held that this language was ambiguous and might simply allow exclusions of "named drivers." The Court was not sure whether the CALIA plainly allowed, or disallowed, coverage exclusions.

However, the Court believed that, even without the desired statutory clarity, the Court could determine whether a certain exclusion violated the underlying "policy of the law." Id. at ¶16, 39 P.3d 771. They found that the purpose of the CALIA was to protect the public from the negligent operation of automobiles, and that, "To effectuate this policy, any vehicle operating on the roads of this state must be secured against liability to innocent victims in the event harm occurs from its negligent operation." Insurance exclusions that violate this public policy must be found invalid.

The Court looked at the *Hartline* exclusion and noted that a "family exclusion" of this sort would "potentially affect a sizable portion of Oklahoma's population." The Court noted that other courts had either completely validated, or completely invalidated "named insured and household exclusions." The *Hartline* Court did neither, but came up with an interesting solution. The Court noted that UM coverage was also meant to protect the victims of automobile accidents. The Court held that "the household and named insured/insured exclusions are invalid only when they operate to deny all coverage to an injured resident family member" and that it will be the responsibility of the Liability insurer to determine whether the exclusion will have the effect of leaving the injured named insured or family member with less than $10,000 in coverage (either from UM or Liability). The Liability insurer must examine whether there are other sources of recovery, such as UM from other vehicles, or other Liability policies.

§5:2

If the exclusion is invalid, the policy will provide Liability coverage "to the very limit of the insured's liability protection." But, the insurer can avoid this rule with proper policy language.

In previous cases the Court had held that if an exclusion were held invalid because of the CALIA, then the policy would be required to provide the statutory minimum Liability coverage of $10,000. However, the Hartline Court made this interesting comment: "Absent some explicit provision in the policy which affords them the minimum protection, wrongly excluded persons -- persons not secured by uninsured motorist coverage -- will be deemed insured to the very limit of the insured's liability protection." This does at least two things: 1) it means that if an exclusion is held invalid under the *Hartline* test, then the claimant is potentially entitled to recover the full policy limits (for example, $100,000), rather than be limited to the minimum $10,000 required by the CALIA; and 2) it allows a Liability insurer to avoid this result with some "explicit provision in the policy" that grants such claimants "the minimum protection" (i.e., $10,000).

In order to allow insurers to adapt to this new rule, the Court held that *Hartline* would not go into effect until one year after the date of the mandate. That makes *Hartline* effective for claims that arise after May 25, 2002. Presumably, insurers will use the time to adjust their investigation procedures and to write new policy language that reduces their "household exclusion" exposure to $10,000.

The *Hartline* decision is interesting in that it does appear to be (despite Justice Opala's explanations) an example of judicial legislation. In any event, if we presume that the household exclusion was invalid before *Hartline*, then, at least as to the household exclusion, what *Hartline* accomplished was to 1) completely validate the exclusion if there are other sources of recovery (such as UM coverage), or 2) if there are no other sources, then the Liability insurer will be liable for its full policy limit (unless it has adopted policy language to limit payment to $10,000/20,000).

As to Liability exclusions other than the household exclusion, it will be interesting to see how, or if, the Court applies the *Hartline* test. The *Hartline* test involves a judicial examination as to whether a certain exclusion somehow violates public policy (*Hartline* at ¶18), but not all exclusions will be invalidated, because the Court recognizes some room for freedom of contract (¶17). Will the Court then re-examine other exclusions (such as the underage driver exclusion in *Young v Mid-Continent Cas. Co.*, 1987 OK 88, 743 P.2d 1084) and make new determinations as to their validity?

Cases arising before *Hartline*.

For cases arising before the effective date of *Hartline,* the Court has reaffirmed that the household exclusion is invalid, but only up to the minimum coverage required under the CALI. *Gordon v Gordon*, 2002 OK 5, 41 P.3d 391. A minor Child was injured while a passenger in a vehicle driven by Mother. Child sought the full $100,000 Liability coverage available on the vehicle involved in the accident as well as stacking of the Liability coverage on another household vehicle not involved in the accident. As to the question of the household exclusion, the Court reaffirmed the holding in *Nation v. State Farm Ins. Co.*, 1994 OK 54, 880 P.2d 877 that the "household exclusion" was against Oklahoma public policy, but that this only applied to amounts up to $10,000. The household exclusion could validly operate to exclude Liability coverage for amounts over $10,000. Further, the Court held that language in the "other insurance" and the "limits of liability" sections of the Liability policies validly prohibited stacking of the Liability policies. *Hartline v. Hartline*, 2001 OK 15, 39 P.3d 765 did not play a part, because the *Gordon* case arose in 1993, well before the date *Hartline* went into effect. See *Gordon*, fn. 1.

§5:3 Exclusion for "bodily injury and property damage caused intentionally by or at the direction of the insured."

See *Equity Ins. v Garrett*, 2008 OK CIV APP 23, 178 P.3d 201, discussed in §2:3 above.

§5:6 Care, Custody or Control Exclusion, or

Property Which the Insured is "In Charge Of."

In *Tapp v Perciful*, 2005 OK 49, 120 P.3d 480 the Court held that the Compulsory Liability Insurance Act invalidated the business auto exclusion. Of course, if an exclusion is invalidated under the CLIA, the exclusion is only inoperative as to the amount of coverage required by the CLIA. In Tapp, the amount required by the CLIA was $10,000, so the Court held that the insurer must provide $10,000 in coverage, despite the exclusion. The current CLIA coverage requirement is $25,000.

§5:7 The "Other Business" Exclusion.

The Tenth Circuit applied the business pursuits exclusion in *Grain Dealers Mut. Ins. Co. v Farmers Alliance Mut. Ins. Co.*, 298 F.3d 1178 (10th Cir. 2002). The McQuarys owned a business called R&M Fleet Services. This business contracted with a third party to dispose of fly ash on the McQuary's land. This land, which also served as their residence, was covered by a homeowners policy issued by Farmers Alliance. The business, R&M Fleet Services, was insured with Grain Dealers. A neighbor of the McQuarys sued the McQuarys because fly ash was washing onto the neighbor's property. Grain Dealers defended the case, but sued Farmers Alliance to share in defense costs. Farmers Alliance defended the claim based, in part, on a "business pursuits" exclusion in their policy. The

Court held that there was no coverage under the Farmers Alliance policy because the claim arose out of the McQuary's business pursuits. Even though this was an incorporated business, the Court held that the suit still arose out of a profit making venture, and that, "An employee's role in a business pursuit is sufficient to bring the employee within the exclusion's scope, given that "business" is defined as "a trade, profession or occupation." *Id.* at 1182.

In *Bailey v Farmers Ins. Co.*, 2006 OK CIV APP 85, 137 P.3d 1260, the Court held that a business pursuits exclusion in a fire policy would apply to a barn where the insured kept and sold horses. Despite the fact that the insured reported profit and loss on the "business" on their taxes, the insured argued that it was only a hobby. Of course, this case deals with a fire policy, but it may be instructive for auto policies.

§5:10 The named driver exclusion.

The holding in *Pierce* was applied to an Uninsured Motorist provision in *O'Brien v Dorrough*, 1996 OK CIV APP 25, 928 P.2d 322. The Driver was excluded from coverage under her step-father's auto policy by means of a "named driver exclusion." Driver was injured by an uninsured motorist as she was operating the step-father's vehicle. She made claim against her step-father's UM policy, arguing that the named driver exclusion could not validly destroy her right to collect UM under the policy. The Court of Appeals disagreed, citing the plain, broad language of the named driver exclusion: "It is agreed that the insurance afforded by this policy shall not apply with respect to any loss arising from any occurrence while any automobile is being operated by or in the care, custody or control of Shannon O'Brien." See §§6:34, 6:49.

The *Pierce* holding was also applied to a Medical Payments provision in *Robinson v GEICO General Ins. Co.*, 1996 OK CIV APP 130, 928 P.2d 971. The GEICO policy contained a general "named driver exclusion" barring any coverage for a certain driver. The Court of Appeals held that this was valid and would apply to bar Medical Payments coverage for the named driver. See §7:17.

The validity of the named driver exclusion was again challenged in *McElmurry v. Garbow,* 2005 OK CIV APP 38, 116 P.3d 198, 201 which held that a policy provision naming the policy holder as an excluded driver violates public policy and is invalid to the extent that it denies liability coverage to innocent third parties. The *McElmurry* Court distinguished this situation from the one in *Pierce v Oklahoma Property and Casualty Ins. Co.*, 1995 OK 78, 901 P.2d 819 (discussed in the main volume) because in *McElmurry* the named driver exclusion purported to exclude the only named insured on the policy. The COCA also seemed to question the continued validity of the Pierce decision in light of more recent Supreme Court decisions invalidating Auto Liability policy exclusions up to the amount required by the Compulsory Liability Insurance Act.

In *Alternative Medicine of Tulsa, Inc. v Cates,* 2006 OK CIV APP 65, 136 P.3d 716, the Court of Civil Appeals invalidated a named driver exclusion at least so far as it defeated UM coverage for innocent third parties riding in the vehicle driven by the excluded driver. For discussion of such exclusions and how they affect UM coverage, see *§*6:49.

The Supreme Court finally weighed in again on the named driver exclusion in *Mulford v Neal,* 2011 OK 20, 264 P.3d 1173. The Court narrowed the circumstances where the named driver exclusion will be allowed. In *Mulford*, the carrier argued that the exclusion was valid because teenagers, as an age class, typically were high-risk. The Court rejected this argument and noted the holding in *Pierce v. Oklahoma Property & Casualty Ins. Co.*, 1995 OK 78, 901 P.2d 819, was limited to those policies where the company has issued a named driver exclusion endorsement because of the "poor driving record of the excluded individual." The named driver exclusion in *Mulford* was not consistent with the public policy expressed in Oklahoma's compulsory insurance law and may not be enforced against injured parties, at least up to the minimum required compulsory coverage.

§5:15 Other Exclusions.

The "Loaned Vehicle Exclusion" in a Garage Policy was discussed in *Ball v Wilshire Ins. Co.*, 2009 OK 38, 221 P.3d 717. The garage owner loaned a vehicle to a customer while the customer's car was being repaired. Wilshire denied Liability and UM coverage on the vehicle after it was involved in an accident while being driven by a customer because the policy had an exclusion which denied coverage to customers driving the vehicle while the customer's auto is being repaired. The Court held that the exclusion was invalid under the Compulsory Liability Insurance Act, which meant that the insurer would have to provide at least the minimum statutory coverage for the vehicle.

§5:16 Business Auto Policies: Operations Exclusion [new]

Federal Ins. Co. v Tri-State Ins. Co., 157 F.3d 800 (10th Cir. Okla 1998) was a declaratory judgment action brought by a General Liability insurer to recover indemnification from another insurer who had issued a Business Auto Policy. An explosion occurred when the operator of a truck stopped to pump material from a storage tank. The truck's engines were running and fumes caused the explosion which burned the truck operators. One of the issues was whether the "Operations Exclusion" in the Business Auto Policy would apply. This clause denied coverage if the bodily injury was "arising out of the operation of" certain equipment that was listed in the policy. One of the banned pieces of equipment was a "pump." The Court of Appeals noted that the fire was caused when a vacuum pump on the truck pulled fumes out of the tank and the fumes were ignited by the engine. Under those facts, did the injury "arise out of" the use of the pump? If it did, there would be no coverage.

The Court said that Oklahoma did not require that an item be the actual "proximate cause" of an injury before that injury could be said to "arise out of" the use of the item. Rather, Oklahoma has adopted a "chain of events" test, as described in §4.11 of this work. Since the vacuum pump was in the "chain of events" that led up to the explosion and injury, the Court held that the Operations Exclusion applied, and the Business Auto Policy had no coverage.

§5:17 Exclusions in homeowners and similar policies for use of a motor vehicle. [New]

Homeowners policies, and other types of insurance policies meant to provide Liability coverage for real property, usually contain exclusions meant to prohibit coverage for automobile use. For example, a homeowners insurer does not want to provide auto coverage for the household, at least under the homeowners policy (they may or may not offer a separate auto policy that would provide such coverage). However, the insurer may word the exclusion in a confusing manner, creating "auto" coverage where none was intended. See *Haworth v Jantzen,* 2006 OK 35, 172 P.3d 193, discussed more fully in §2:26, where a perceived "ambiguity" between two phrases in the "motor vehicle" exclusion actually created coverage and turned a farm and ranch liability policy into an auto policy.

However, in general, the Court has been reluctant to extend the coverage of a homeowner's policy to the use of an automobile. For example, in *Phillips v Estate of Greenfield,* 1993 OK 110, 859 P.2d 1101 (discussed in §4:14 in the main volume), the Court held that a homeowner's policy excluded coverage for negligent entrustment claims. Also see *BP America, Inc. v State Auto Prop. & Cas. Ins. Co.*, 2005 OK 65, 148 P.3d 832, where the Court held that a business commercial general liability policy did not provide coverage for an auto accident. The policy contained an exclusion for the use of an auto by "any insured," and thus did not indemnify the named insured for the negligent use of an auto by an additional insured. "Furthermore, adopting the position advanced by the insured would require that we unilaterally convert a general liability policy -- without motor vehicle coverage -- into a automotive liability policy. This we will not do."

Chapter 6: Uninsured Motorist Coverage.

§6:2 Applicability of the UM statute to certain "motor carrier" and "commercial" policies. [New]

36 O.S. §3636 is not applicable to all vehicles. 36 O.S. §3637, as amended in 2004 reads:

> This act shall not apply to any policy covering motor trucks operated by a motor carrier as defined in 47 O.S. 1961, Section 161, as amended, where the named insured has employees who operate motor trucks or to any other commercial automobile liability policy covering motor trucks where the named insured has employees and such employees are covered by workers' compensation on the effective date of the policy.

The effect of this statute is largely unexplored, especially as to commercial auto policies covering "motor trucks," as this language was added in 2004. As to vehicles or policies that come under the definitions in §3637, there is an argument to be made that such vehicles, even if covered by a written "UM" policy, are not sujbect to all of the public policy interpretations of Oklahoma UM policies, since §3636 does not apply to such policies.

§6:15 –The "underinsured" tortfeasor.

§6:15

The tortfeasor covered by an umbrella policy.

In *GEICO Gen. Ins. Co. v Nortwestern Pac. Indem. Co.*, 2005 OK 40, 115 P.3d 856, the Court held that a tortfeasor's umbrella liability policy will not be considered when calculating whether the tortfeasor is uninsured or underinsured. The Court held:

> ¶22 Title 36 O.S. 2001 § 3636 does not contemplate that excess liability policies of the sort issued by NPIC are to be included in determining the "liability limits" of "an insured motor vehicle," as those terms are used in § 3636. Section 3636 applies only to "primary liability policies insuring against liability arising from ownership, maintenance, or operation of an automobile. . . ." *Moser v. Liberty Mutual Ins. Co.*, 1986 OK 78, ¶ 5, n.8, 731 P.2d 406. "The uninsured motorist provisions apply to all automobile liability insurance policies (or motor vehicle liability policies as defined in 47 O.S. § 7-324) but not to 'umbrella' policies. . . ." *Moser* at ¶ 8. [Footnote omitted, emphasis added.] Despite differences in *Moser* from the situation presented here, we clearly stated there that § 3636 does not apply to excess liability policies of the sort at issue here. Thus, we find the *Moser* opinion instructive and hold that § 3636(C) does not apply to excess

liability policies.

§6:17 The "self insured" tortfeasor as "uninsured motorist." [New]

The Court of Civil Appeals is of the opinion that a City owned vehicle, that is permissibly "self insured" under Oklahoma statutes, is not "uninsured." In *Newberry v Allstate Insurance Co.*, 1998 OK CIV APP 139, 963 P.2d 632, the tortfeasor was injured in an accident with a City employee. The City's limit of liability for the tort was $100,000 under the Governmental Tort Claims Act, 51 O.S.Supp.1994 § 154(A)(2). The insured sued Allstate, his UM insurer, claiming that the City, as a "self insured" entity, was completely "uninsured" for UM purposes, since the City had no "Liability insurance." The parties stipulated that the insured suffered $15,000 in damages and submitted the question to the Court. The Court of Civil Appeals held that the provisions of 51 O.S.1991 §§ 159(C), 167(B) indicate a Legislative intent to allow "self-insurance" to work in the stead of actual "Liability insurance." The City would be treated as if it were an insured tortfeasor with $100,000 in coverage. Therefore, the $15,000 claim was adequately covered by the City's self-insured limit.

A similar situation arose in *Carlos v. State Farm Mut. Auto. Ins. Co.*, 1996 OK CIV APP 158, 935 P.2d 1182. There, the question was whether the injured claimant was allowed to assert a claim against her UM coverage after a collision with a state-owned vehicle operated by an employee of the Oklahoma Department of Transportation. The court held she could not, because the amount of her claim was "undisputably less than the liability limits of section 154." *Id.* at 1185.

In discussion, the *Carlos* Court noted the case of *Karlson v. City of Oklahoma City*, 1985 OK 45, 711 P.2d 72. The *Carlos* Court said, "Although not specifically addressing whether the state/political subdivision was considered "uninsured" within section 3636 if the entity did not carry separate liability insurance, the general tenor of Karlson is that waiver of sovereign immunity, up to the liability limits imposed by title 51, is the functional equivalent of insurance to that amount." *Id.* at 1184.

§6:18 Allowing the statute of limitations to run against an otherwise insured tortfeasor does not make the tortfeasor "uninsured." [New]

In *Gates v Eller*, 2001 OK 38, 22 P.3d 1215, the Supreme Court held that allowing the statute of limitations to run against an otherwise insured tortfeasor does not make the tortfeasor an "uninsured motorist." The claimant argued that once the statute of limitations ran against the tortfeasor the tortfeasor's Liability insurance became unavailable and the tortfeasor should be considered to be completely uninsured for purposes of UM calculation. The Supreme Court disagreed. A complete discussion of the *Gates* case is in §6:36.

§6:19 Settlement for less than tortfeasor's limits [New]

In *Porter v State Farm Mut. Auto. Ins. Co.*, 2010 OK CIV APP 8, 231 P.3d 691, the Court of Civil Appeals held that Plaintiff's settlement with the tortfeasor can cause Plaintiff to lose her ability to collect UM coverage if the settlement is for less than the Liability limits available to the tortfeasor. The Court held that, when Plaintiff gave the tortfeasor a full release, for payment of $85,000 on a $100,000 Liability policy, the Plaintiff was no longer "legally entitled to recover" against the tortfeasor. Since the Plaintiff must be able to establish that she is legally entitled to recover from the tortfeasor, the Plaintiff would not be able to prove that element of her UM claim. The Court also held that the settlement for $85,000 established that the value of Plaintiff's claim was less than the amount of the tortfeasor's Liability policy, so Plaintiff could not prove the other element of a UM claim, that the value of Plaintiff's claim exceeded the amount of the tortfeasor's Liability policy (i.e.: the Plaintiff could not establish that the tortfeasor was "underinsured").

§6:30 Operation of motor vehicle and causation.

This question came up again in *Whitmire v Mid-Continent Cas. Co.*, 1996 OK CIV APP 116, 928

P.2d 959. The insured was abducted from her house and taken, in the insured vehicle, to a bridge crossing where the car was intentionally rolled down an embankment into a tree. The insured was then forced to sit in the front seat of the car as the tortfeasor poured gasoline over her and set her, and the car, on fire. The insured suffered extensive burns. The Court of Appeals held that the tortfeasor was not an "operator" of a motor vehicle at the time she poured gasoline from a can and struck the match. "Such activity was not related to the transportation use of the automobile, "and injury resulting therefrom is not within the UM coverage mandated by § 3636.'" *Id.* at 962. Further, the insured's car was merely the "situs" of the tort, but was not the initial point in the "chain of events" that led to her injury. Judge Hansen filed a strong dissent.

In *Walker v Farmers Ins. Co., Inc.*, 83 F.3d 349 (10th Cir. 1996) the Court had to deal with a long standing feud that erupted into gunfire. The insured was in his van when it was broadsided by a pickup driven by Perry Enloe. Wayne Enloe, Perry's father then stopped his truck, got a gun and began firing shots. The insured exited his van and ran down the road. He was felled by a bullet, and Wayne Enloe then fired a shot into his head, killing him. The insured surviving spouse made claim under the UM and the Med Pay portions of the Farmers policy. The Tenth Circuit reviewed the tests set up in the *Safeco*, *Willard* and *Byus*, finding that these tests were "inconsistent," fn. 2. However, the Court felt that the same result should be reached here, no matter which test was applied. There were two potential tortfeasors, Perry and Wayne, and both were uninsured. The Court found that Wayne Enloe's actions would not trigger the UM coverage because Wayne's only used his vehicle to get to the scene of the prior accident between Perry and the insured. Wayne's vehicle was not used to injure the insured. However, Perry's vehicle was the cause of the initial auto accident between Perry and the insured; thus Perry's vehicle usage was tied in with the insured's eventual death (even though it was not Perry who shot him). However, although Perry Enloe's use of his vehicle was in the chain of events that led to the insured's death, the Court refused to find that the use of that vehicle actually caused the death. It was not foreseeable to Perry that the accident between himself and the insured would cause Wayne to shoot the insured. Therefore, the shooting broke the chain of causation between the "accident" and the shooting.

The question arose again in *Mayer v State Farm Mut. Auto. Ins. Co.*, 1997 OK 67, 944 P.2d 288. This case arose out of the bombing of the Murrah Building. The claimant was injured in the bombing and made a UM claim against his own insurer. The Supreme Court held that, at the time the bomb exploded, the van used to house the bomb was simply being used as a "launching pad" for the bomb. It was no longer being used in its "transportation" mode, and the driver of the van had apparently abandoned it prior to the bomb exploding. For another similar case, arising out of the bombing of the Murrah Building, see *Nichols v Nationwide Mutual Ins. Co.*, 948 F.Supp. 988 (W.D.Ok. 1996).

Also, see *Ply v National Union Fire Ins. Co.*, 2003 OK 97, 81 P.3d 643, below.

Recovering because of a tortfeasor's negligent "maintenance" of an uninsured motor vehicle.

In *Ply v National Union Fire Ins. Co.*, 2003 OK 97, 81 P.3d 643, the Court held that when an employer provides faulty or negligent instructions or directions to an employee relating to the use of an employer-owned motor vehicle and the employee is injured while following the instructions, then the employer's negligence will be sufficient "control" over the vehicle to qualify as negligent "operation" on the employer's part. Even though the employer was not present when the accident happened, the employer's assertion of control over the manner that the vehicle was to be used was sufficient to qualify the employer as a tortfeasor who was "operating" the vehicle. Further, the employer qualified as a negligent "owner" of the uninsured vehicle under 36 O.S. §3636.

The Court also noted that the Plaintiff alleged that the employer was negligent in the employer's "maintenance" of the vehicle being used by the injured employee. This negligent "maintenance" occurred prior to the accident (employer failed to repair a leaky hydraulic line). The Court held that this negligent maintenance by the employer was sufficient to make the employer an "uninsured tortfeasor" under §3636. The Court relied on the language in §3636(A) which required that UM coverage be offered in conjunction with Liability policies, when the Liability policies provide protection for "ownership, maintenance or use" of a motor vehicle. The insurer argued that the "maintenance" language in the statute referred to injuries that occurred during the performance of maintenance functions on the vehicle. The Court disagreed and held that it could also apply to a vehicle that malfunctions, causing injury, as the result of negligent failure to maintain the vehicle.

§6:32 Who is an Insured Person under Uninsured Motorist Coverage? Only an "insured person" under a policy can claim the right to "stack" that policy.

<u>The validity of the named driver exclusion.</u>

The Supreme Court has determined that an auto Liability insurer is entitled to exclude named individuals from coverage by using a "named driver endorsement." See *Pierce v Oklahoma Property and Casualty Ins. Co.*, 1995 OK 78, 901 P.2d 819, discussed at §5:10 in the main volume. The holding in *Pierce* was applied to an Uninsured Motorist provision in *O'Brien v Dorrough*, 1996 OK CIV APP 25, 928 P.2d 322. The Driver was excluded from coverage under her step-father's auto policy by means of a "named driver exclusion." Driver was injured by an uninsured motorist as she was operating the step-father's vehicle. She made claim against her step-father's UM policy, arguing that the named driver exclusion could not validly destroy her right to collect UM under the policy. The Court of Appeals disagreed, citing the plain, broad language of the named driver exclusion: "It is agreed that the insurance afforded by this policy shall not apply with respect to any loss arising from any occurrence while any automobile is being operated by or in the care, custody or control of Shannon O'Brien." Further, the Court noted that §3636(B) required a UM policy to only cover those persons who are insured under the underlying Liability policy, *Id.* at 325. See §6:49.

Employees do not have to be defined "insureds" under their employer's UM policy.

Graham v Travelers Ins. Co., 2002 OK 95, 61 P.3d 225 involved an employee who was injured in an accident while he was driving his own vehicle on his employer's business. The employer had a liability insurance policy that provided coverage for employee's vehicles while being used on the employer's business. However, the employer's policy did not expressly extend UM coverage to employee's vehicles while being used on the employer's business. The employee argued that §3636 required that every vehicle covered by a liability insurance policy must also be covered by UM coverage. The insured argued that, since the employer's insurer had agreed to provide liability coverage to the employee's vehicle in this instance, it must also provide UM coverage. The Supreme Court disagreed. The Court held that the owner of the policy, and the insurer, had negotiated for an extension of liability insurance coverage to cover the employee's vehicles being used on company business but that, at the same time, they agreed to a contractual limitation that UM coverage would not be so extended. This was contractual limitation was valid under Oklahoma law. The Court equated this situation to the case of *Shepard v Farmers Ins. Co., Inc.*, 1983 OK 103, 678 P.2d 250, where the Court held that the insurer was free to determine, in the first instance, who it would and would not provide UM insurance to. In this case the insurer had bargained to provide liability coverage to it's insured's employees who were using their vehicles on company business; however, it had not bargained to provide UM coverage to such employees.

For another case similar to *Graham*, see *National American Ins. Co. v Vallion*, 2008 OK CIV APP 41, 183 P.3d 175.

Commercial UM policies, issued to named insured corporations, are not ambiguous simply because

the policies sometimes refer to "family members."

In *American Economy Ins. Co. v Bogdahn*, 2004 OK 9, 89 P.3d 1051, American's UM policy was issued to a family owned corporation (a pharmacy) as named insured. The pharmacist's child was injured while riding an uninsured all terrain vehicle. The question was whether the child was an "insured" under the pharmacy's UM policy. The UM policy defined "insured" as "If you are an individual, any 'family member.'" The term "family member" was defined as "a person related to you by blood, marriage or adoption who is a resident of your household, including a ward or foster child." The term "you" refers to "the Named Insured" (i.e.: the pharmacy). Obviously, since the pharmacy was not an "individual" (it was a corporation), it was incapable of having "family members." The Court held that this was not ambiguous, and that the child was not entitled to coverage under the pharmacy's UM policy.

In *Haberman v The Hartford Ins. Group*, 443 F.3d 1257 (10th Cir., 2006), the named insured on a Hartford commercial policy was a professional corporation. However, Haberman, the owner of the corporation, was listed by name, in a "Named Persons Endorsement." The Endorsement said that it "modifies insurance provided under the...Business Auto Coverage Form" and that Haberman is an "'insured' for Liability Coverage" under the "Liability

Coverage" section of the policy. Haberman was involved in an accident in a friend's vehicle and made a UM claim against the Hartford policy. Hartford argued that the Endorsement extended coverage to Haberman individually only under the Liability policy. However, the Tenth Circuit held that the language of the Endorsement plainly extended Haberman coverage under the entire Business Auto Coverage or, in the alternative, was at least ambiguous and could be read to extend coverage to Haberman to the entire Business Auto Coverage, which would include UM. The Tenth Circuit further held that, once it was determined that Haberman was a defined insured under the UM portion of the Hartford policy, Haberman was then entitled to "stack" the UM coverage available on the two vehicles covered under the Hartford polciy. This case is also discussed in §§1:2, 2:2, and 6:77.

The practitioner should also examine 36 O.S. §3637, noted in §6.2, and determine whether the commercial policy in question is even covered under the UM statute.

A person who is otherwise a defined "insured" can not recover for derivative damages sustained because of the death of a person who is not a defined "insured."

In *London v Farmers Ins. Co., Inc.*, 2003 OK CIV APP 10, 63 P.3d 552, the Court of Civil Appeals held that an insured under a UM policy was not entitled to recover for the death of a person who was not an insured. The insured was the father's minor child. However, the child was not living with the father, but with the child's grandmother. The father was killed in a motorcycle accident. The grandmother, on child's behalf, made claim against her UM coverage for the father's death. Since the father was not an "insured person" under the grandmother's policy, Farmers was not obligated to pay UM benefits for the father's death, even though the child was living in the grandmother's household.

§6:33 When is the insured "legally entitled to recover" against the uninsured motorist?

The Supreme Court has decided that a child of "tender years" is incapable of negligence and therefore can not be a "tortfeasor" in a UM case. In *Martin v. Hartford Underwriters Ins. Co.*, 1996 OK 55, 918 P.2d 49, the insured was injured when her three-year-old child unexpectedly pulled car into gear as the insured was trying to enter. The insured was not "legally entitled to recover" damages from alleged uninsured motorist child since child, at three years of age, was incapable of negligence as matter of law.

In *Ply v National Union Fire Ins. Co.*, 2003 OK 97, 81 P.3d 643, the Court held that an employee is "legally entitled to recover" from an employer, for UM purposes, where a supervisor, acting on behalf of the employer, provides faulty or negligent instructions or directions to an employee relation to the use of an employer-owned motor vehicle and the employee is injured while following the instructions. Even though the employer is immune from the employee's tort claim, because of the Workers Compensation Act, the employer's actions (negligently instructing the employee in the use of the vehicle; negligent maintenance of the vehicle) are sufficient to fulfill the "legally entitled to recover" element of the employee's UM claim.

Settlement for less than tortfeasor's limits.

In *Porter v State Farm Mut. Auto. Ins. Co.*, 2010 OK CIV APP 8, 231 P.3d 691, the Court of Civil Appeals held that Plaintiff's settlement with the tortfeasor can cause Plaintiff to lose her ability to collect UM coverage if the settlement is for less than the Liability limits available to the tortfeasor. The Court held that, when Plaintiff gave the tortfeasor a full release, for payment of $85,000 on a $100,000 Liability policy, the Plaintiff was no longer "legally entitled to recover" against the tortfeasor. Since the Plaintiff must be able to establish that she is legally entitled to recover from the tortfeasor, the Plaintiff would not be able to prove that element of her UM claim. The Court also held that the settlement for $85,000 established that the value of Plaintiff's claim was less than the amount of the tortfeasor's Liability policy, so Plaintiff could not prove the other element of a UM claim, that the value of Plaintiff's claim exceeded the amount of the tortfeasor's Liability policy (i.e.: the Plaintiff could not establish that the tortfeasor was "underinsured").

§6:35 What measure of damages can be recovered against the UM carrier?

§6:36 -Determining damages in relationship to available liability insurance. UM coverage as "primary." "Exhaustion" of liability coverage.

For a discussion of an important case regarding the "exhaustion" requirement, see *Mustain v United States Fidelity and Guaranty Co.*, 1996 OK 98, 925 P.2d 533, in which the Supreme Court generally declared that, as between the insurer and the insured, all UM coverage is "primary," and an "excess" UM insurer can not withhold payment waiting for a "primary" UM insurer to complete payment. See the full discussion in §6:80.

On December 22, 1998, the Supreme Court, in a 5-4 opinion, issued *Burch v Allstate Ins. Co.*, 1998 OK 129, 977 P.2d 1057. This decision has far reaching implications for UM coverage in Oklahoma. The decision purports to clarify the role of UM coverage and how a UM carrier's obligations are calculated under Oklahoma law. Although it does clarify some issues, it also creates some ambiguities, and creates new procedural issues for further litigation.

The facts of *Burch* are somewhat unique. The claimant was a passenger in her own vehicle, with her husband at the wheel. She was injured in a one-car accident, meaning that her husband was the "tortfeasor." One day before the statute of limitations would have run on the tort claim against her husband, she filed a lawsuit against Allstate, her UM carrier. Of course, Allstate was also the Liability carrier for her tortfeasor husband. The tortfeasor's Liability insurance limits were $10,000 (because of a "step-down" provision in the Allstate policy) and the UM coverage available to the claimant for her injuries was $100,000. Allstate and the claimant stipulated that her damages were $50,000.

The statute of limitations had run against the tortfeasor, and Allstate's $10,000 in "Liability" money was no longer actually available to the claimant. The insured claimant took the position that she was entitled to collect her entire $50,000 loss against Allstate's UM policy. However, Allstate argued, under *Buzzard v. Farmers Insurance Co.*, 1991 OK 127, 824 P.2d 1105, that it was only obligated to pay those amounts of damages that exceed the tortfeasor's Liability insurance. Therefore, Allstate's position was that it was only obligated to pay $40,000 ($50,000 damages - $10,000 Liability insurance), and that it made no difference that this Liability insurance was no longer "available" to the insured, since the insured was the one who allowed the statute of limitations to expire.

The Western District of Oklahoma agreed with Allstate, and found, under *Buzzard*, that Allstate was only liable for $40,000. The insured appealed the case to the Tenth Circuit Court of Appeals. The Tenth Circuit sent the following "certified question" to the Oklahoma Supreme Court: "When an insured's damages in an automobile accident exceed a tortfeasor's liability limits and the insured seeks payment for damages directly from its underinsured motorist (UIM) carrier, is the UIM carrier liable for the entire amount of the insured's claim when the liability and UIM coverage are provided by the same carrier but the statute of limitations period has expired on the liability claim?"

The Oklahoma Supreme Court answered the question in the affirmative, but not before it did a general review of Oklahoma UM law, and a refutation of some so-called "dicta" in the *Buzzard* case.

The Court first noted that UM coverage is "primary" in relationship to the tortfeasor's Liability insurance. The Court has previously held that UM coverage was "primary" in relationship to other available UM coverage. *Mustain v. United States Fidelity and Guaranty Co.*, 1996 OK 98, 925 P.2d 533, discussed in §6:80 of this Supplement. However, it had not previously expressly declared that UM was "primary" in relationship to the tortfeasor's Liability insurance. As the Court said in footnote 3 of the *Burch* opinion, "Primary coverage is defined as that for which, 'under the terms of the policy, the insurer is liable without regard to any other insurance coverage available.'.... In the law of general liability insurance, primary insurance is defined as that which pays a policyholder's first-dollar damages and is the first policy in line to pay such damages." To the Court, this meant "that an uninsured motorist carrier is liable for the entire amount of its insured's loss from the first dollar up to the UM policy limits without regard to the presence of any other insurance." *Id* at §2, emphasis added.

However, the Court's previous *Buzzard* opinion seemed to contradict this holding. In *Buzzard*, the Court said that a UM carrier was only obligated pay "that amount of injury or damage which exceeds the liability limits of the tortfeasor." *Buzzard*, 1991 OK 127 at ¶24, 824 P.2d at 1111. The *Burch* Court frankly admitted that it had mis-stated the law in *Buzzard*, and that this language in *Buzzard* was "pure *obiter dictum.*" *Burch* at ¶12.

The *Burch* opinion also says that 36 O.S. §3636 only mandates one kind of UM coverage, and that is "uninsured" coverage. A tortfeasor's "underinsured" status is only one way that a motorist can become "uninsured." "§3636 creates only uninsured motorist coverage, and includes within that term both motor vehicles on which their owners carry no insurance as well as those on which their owners' coverage is in an amount insufficient to satisfy a loss." Therefore, it makes no difference, in calculating the amount due by the UM insurer, whether the tortfeasor had Liability insurance or not.

Does that mean that the injured claimant can make a claim against the UM insurer even when the claimant's damages do not exceed the available liability insurance? The answer to this question is still somewhat ambiguous under the *Burch* opinion, and we can expect different positions to be taken. However, in this writer's opinion, the injured claimant must still prove that her damages exceed the available Liability insurance before a UM claim is even payable. This belief is confirmed by the Court's subsequent ruling in the *Gates* case, discussed below. However, once it is shown that the damages do exceed this amount, then the UM insurer is liable for the entire amount of the damages, up to the UM policy limits, without regard to the amount of the Liability insurance. The Court said:

> The insured who has paid a premium for uninsured motorist coverage and presses a claim for the actual amount of damages sustained within the policy limits seeks no more than recovery of that for which the premium was paid. If the liability limits of a motor vehicle are less than the amount of the injured insured's claim, that vehicle is classified as *uninsured*. Based on this definition, one can conclude that under our statutory scheme, the UM carrier's obligation to its insured is *identical* regardless of the underlying reason for the classification of the vehicle as uninsured. We hold §3636

> mandates that when the preconditions for the loss under uninsured motorist coverage exist, an uninsured motorist coverage carrier is obligated to pay the entire loss of its injured insured from the first dollar up to the policy limits.
>
> *Id* at §13, emphasis added.

Therefore, the amount of the tortfeasor's Liability insurance is still important because the claimant must still show that her claim exceeds the amount of the available Liability insurance.

The *Burch* opinion also could be interpreted to hold that a tortfeasor's Liability insurance becomes "unavailable," for purposes of this calculation, when the statute of limitations runs against an un-sued tortfeasor. That was certainly argued by the Plaintiff. However, there may be some question whether the *Burch* Court actually reached this issue. The Burch's damages exceeded the tortfeasor's Liability insurance. Under the *Burch* rule, Allstate would be required to pay from its UM policy because of that fact alone. Under the rule set forth in *Burch*, it makes little difference, to the Plaintiff in *Burch*, whether or not the statute of limitations has run against the tortfeasor. Burch is entitled to UM coverage simply because her damages exceed the tortfeasor's Liability insurance limits. The running of the statute of limitations against the tortfeasor would not improve Burch's position against Allstate.

Therefore, any language in *Burch* that hints

that a tortfeasor may become "uninsured" simply because the tort statute of limitations may have run against him, could well be "dicta." The *Burch* Court did not have to reach the question of the statute of limitations in order to make its decision in *Burch*. However, some will argue that the underlying logic of the *Burch* decision will require a holding that the running of the statute of limitations against a tortfeasor makes that tortfeasor's Liability insurance "unavailable" for purposes of UM calculation.

The import of such a holding, if indeed that is the "holding" of *Burch*, is that the "uninsured" status of the tortfeasor, and thus the amount owed by the UM insurer, can change from day to day. For example, the day before the statute of limitations runs, the UM insurer may not owe anything, since the tortfeasor's Liability insurance exceeds the claimant's damages. However, the next day, after the statute of limitations runs against the un-sued tortfeasor, the UM insurer suddenly becomes liable for the full amount of the loss (up to the UM limits). However, again, we believe the Court cleared up this argument by its ruling in the *Gates* case, discussed below.

The practical implications of the *Burch* case, including the suspect "statute of limitations holding," can be seen by exploring a few scenarios:

1. Presume the claimant has $50,000 in damages and the tortfeasor has $10,000 in Liability insurance. The UM insurer has $100,000 in UM coverage. The claimant files suit against the UM insurer and the tortfeasor before the statute of

limitations expires and the UM insurer brings a subrogation cross-claim against the tortfeasor. Result: The UM insurer is obligated to pay $50,000 to the claimant and continue pursuing the tortfeasor for subrogation to recover the $10,000 Liability insurance, as well as any damages it can recover from the tortfeasor personally.

2. Presume the same scenario as in 1, except that the claimant files suit only against the UM insurer and the UM insurer does not file suit against the tortfeasor before the statute of limitations runs. Result: The UM insurer is still obligated to pay $50,000 to the claimant, even though it can no longer pursue subrogation against the tortfeasor.

3. Presume the same scenario as in 1, except that the claimant files suit only against the UM insurer before the two year statute of limitations has run and the UM insurer attempts to bring in the tortfeasor by "third party" petition in order to assert its subrogation rights. Result: The UM insurer is still obligated to pay $50,000 to the claimant. Can the UM insurer still pursue its' subrogation claim? There may be an argument that the UM insurer does not have standing to file a subrogation action when the insurer has not yet made a payment and the insured has not filed suit against the tortfeasor. Even if the UM insurer does have "standing" to bring the action, how will the eventual lawsuit be tried before the jury? Claimant vs UM insurer, with the tortfeasor present and bound by the verdict? Claimant vs UM insurer, with the tortfeasor not present (because of perceived

"prejudice") and therefore not bound by the verdict? Claimant vs tortfeasor, despite the fact that the claimant has not sued the tortfeasor?

4. Presume the claimant has $50,000 in damages and the tortfeasor has $1,000,000 in Liability insurance. The UM insurer has $100,000 in UM coverage.. Under *Burch*, the day before the tort statute of limitations ran, the UM insurer is obliged to pay nothing because the Liability insurance is sufficient to pay the claim. The "preconditions" for UM coverage have not been met, and the UM insurer does not have to make any payment. However, the day after the tort statute of limitations has run, with the tortfeasor un-sued, the UM insurer suddenly becomes liable to pay its entire $50,000 in UM coverage because the Liability insurance is no longer "available." The UM insurer has no right of subrogation because the tort statute of limitations has run against the tortfeasor. However, the Court's ruling in *Gates*, discussed below, clears up this problem. *Gates* holds that the running of the statute of limitations does not make the tortfeasor's Liability insurance "unavailable" and that, under this scenario, the claimant could not collect UM because he could not show that the tortfeasor was an "uninsured motorist."

5. Presume the same scenario as in 1 or 4, except that the claimant does not file suit against anyone before the two year tort statute of limitations has run. The claimant is secure in the knowledge that the UM statute of limitations is five years and that, as

soon as the two years runs, she will have a direct claim against her UM carrier for the full amount of her damages under *Burch*. As the statute of limitations approaches, the UM insurer wants to preserve its subrogation rights, so it sues the tortfeasor. Again, the same questions, as in 3, arise: does the UM insurer have standing to bring such an action; can the court push "UM insurer vs tortfeasor" to trial before the UM claimant concludes her claim against the UM insurer?

These, and other, scenarios will likely come up in litigation. The *Burch* case has changed some of our thinking about UM coverage. The *Burch* case left some questions that have been argued by some counsel. For example, does the running of the tort statute of limitations actually make the tortfeasor's Liability insurance "unavailable" for UM calculations. Does the UM carrier owe "first dollar" even when the damages do not exceed the available Liability insurance? This writer believes that these questions have been answered in the *Gates* case discussed below. It also remains to be seen how the Court will react to some of the procedural questions that will appear as both Plaintiff and Defense counsel plot new "strategies" for handling UM lawsuits.

Burch mentions, and disapproves of, *Smith v American Fidelity Ins. Co.*. 1998 OK CIV APP 70, 963 P.2d 16. Here is the *Burch* Court's description of the *Smith* case:

> In *Smith*, the insured made demand for

> payment of her entire damages (in the amount of $12,000) from her UM carrier, although the negligent party had $10,000 in collectible liability insurance. The insured argued that once the preconditions for the application of §3636 are met, a UM carrier is liable to its insured for the entire amount of the insured's claim up to the UM policy limits, even if liability insurance remains available. The insurer interposed *Buzzard*. The court agreed with the insurer, holding that under *Buzzard* the insurer cannot be compelled to pay the insured's entire damage claim where the tortfeasor's liability insurance remains available.

Needless to say, the *Burch* Court disagreed with the holding of the *Smith* case.

In *Reeder v American Economy Ins. Co.*, 88 F.3d 892 (10th Cir. 1996), the Tenth Circuit has held that an insurer's settlement offer, made under *Buzzard v Farmers Ins. Co.*, is not admissible against the insurer in a subsequent "bad faith" case. Even though the duty of "good faith" requires the insurer to make such an evaluation and offer, it is still a settlement offer under Evidence Rule 408, and is not admissible. Further, the Court held that an insurer's evaluation and offer made three months after their contractual liability was legally determined by the Court (even though it was twenty-one months after the UM claim was filed) was in “good faith” as a matter of law, since there had been a serious dispute as to coverage.

Gates v Eller, 2001 OK 38, 22 P.3d 1215 confirmed that the *Burch* opinion does not mean that every UM claimant can completely ignore the tortfeasor’s Liability insurance. An accident occurred between the Gates vehicle and the Eller vehicle. Eller had $25,000/50,000 Liability coverage. After the statute of limitations expired against the tortfeasor, the insured brought an action against Eller and Gate's UM insurer, Prudential. Actions against Eller were subsequently dismissed because of the running of the statute of limitations. Plaintiffs conceded that their damages did not exceed the amount of Eller's Liability coverage. The UM insurer argued that this meant that Gates had no UM claim. Gates argued that the running of the statute of limitations against Eller essentially made Eller's Liability coverage "unavailable," meaning that Eller should be considered as "uninsured." The Supreme Court disagreed with Gates, holding that an insured motor vehicle, such as Eller's, did not become an "uninsured motor vehicle" simply because the insureds allowed the statute of limitations to run against the tortfeasor.

Plaintiffs relied on *Burch v. Allstate Insurance Co.*, 1998 OK 129, 977 P.2d 1057 for the general proposition that a UM insurer is liable for the "first dollar" of damages payable under a UM claim, not just for those damages that exceed the Liability coverage. In other words they argued that, under *Burch*, Prudential was obligated to pay Plaintiff's damages and it was up to Prudential to pursue the tortfeasor for subrogation. The Supreme Court disagreed, and explained it's ruling in *Burch* (emphasis in original):

> "¶ 12 Our uninsured motorist statute imposes upon an injured insured seeking to recover uninsured motorist insurance benefits the burden of proving the uninsured status of the tortfeasor's motor vehicle. Our holding in *Burch* did not diminish this burden in any respect. To the contrary, Burch observed that an injured insured must demonstrate that the **preconditions for loss under the uninsured motorist coverage exist** before he or she can recover under the primary uninsured motorist coverage.

The Court went on to hold that the running of the statute of limitations against the tortfeasor does not mean that the tortfeasor is no longer covered by Liability insurance. This is obvious: the Liability insurance is not destroyed; all that has happened is that the claimant has lost the right to enforce the tort claim against the tortfeasor. The net result may be that the claimant can no longer force payment from the Liability insurer, but that does not mean that the Liability insurance no longer exists.

The Plaintiff also argued that the Court's holding in *Uptegraft v. Home Insurance Company*, 1983 OK 41, 662 P.2d 681 implied that the Plaintiff was allowed to watch the statute of limitations run against the tortfeasor and still pursue a UM claim against the UM insurer. The Court noted that *Uptegraft* did say that the UM insurer could not complain that the claimant had passively destroyed the insurer's subrogation rights by allowing the statute of limitations to expire; but *Uptegraft* did not change the requirement that the insured must still prove that the tortfesor was operating an "uninsured motor vehicle."

Thus, if the claimant allows the statute of limitations to run against the tortfeasor, the claimant might still pursue a UM claim against the UM insurer and require the UM insurer to pay the claim from "first dollar" (*Burch*). However, the UM insurer will owe nothing unless and until the claimant shows that the value of his claim exceeds any Liability insurance that was available to the tortfeasor. The claimant who allows the statute of limitations to run against the tortfeasor runs the risk of recovering nothing from the tortfeasor, and recovering no UM.

Similarly, see *Lamfu v Guideone Ins. Co.*, 2006 OK CIV APP 19, 131 P.3d 712. Plaintiff agreed with the UM insurer that the value of the plaintiff's claim was less than the amount of the tortfeasor's Liability insurance limits. Nevertheless, plaintiff demanded payment under the UM policy.

The COCA held that the UM insurer was not obligated to make any payment on the claim because the agreed value of the claim was less than the Liability insurance limits. The tortfeasor simply did not qualify as an Uninsured Motorist.

§6:38 -UM Coverage for Prejudgment Interest.

In *Gregg v Le Mars Ins. Co.*, 2009 OK CIV APP 93, 227 P.3d 1107, the Court held that the UM insured was entitled to collect prejudgment interest against a UM arbitration award. Prior to the award, the Liability insurer had paid its limits, and another UM insurer had paid its limits. Claim was made against the Le Mars policy. Some settlement discussions were had and Le Mars offered $80,000 of its $300,000 coverage limits to settle the insured. No agreement was reached to settle the UM claim for $80,000, but the insured accepted the $80,000 payment and the parties proceeded to arbitrate whether additional amounts were owed. The arbitration determined that an additional payment of $65,000 was due the insured. The Court determined that the prejudgment interest on the $65,000 award should begin running from the date that the right to UM benefits became "established" which, under these fact, was the date that Le Mars accepted liability for the claim by tendering the $80,000 payment.

§6:42 The application and validity of exclusions in a UM policy.

§6:45 -Exclusion denying coverage when the insured takes a judgment against the tortfeasor, or sues the tortfeasor, without the consent of the UM insurer. The "no action' or "consent to sue" exclusion.

The exclusion was discussed again by the Court of Civil Appeals in *Conner v American Commerce Ins. Co.*, 2009 OK CIV APP 61, 216 P.3d 850. Barry Conner insured his motorcycle with AIG and signed a UM waiver. Barry was a resident of his parent's household. His parents were not insured with AIG but carried their auto coverage with American Commerce Ins. He lived with his parents, so he would qualify as a "resident relative" insured under their American Commerce policy. Further, Barry was a "listed driver" of his parent's vehicles on the American Commerce policy. Barry was involved in an accident on his motorcycle and tried to make a UM claim against his parents insurance policy. American Commerce denied coverage because their policy had an exclusion that excluded UM coverage for any insured "Who is a 'family member,' while 'occupying,' . . . any motor vehicle owned by that person: . . . . b. which is not insured for [UM] coverage."

The Court of Civil Appeals upheld the applicability of the exclusion under these facts. The Court noted that 36 O.S. § 3636 was amended in 2004 to add a new section (E) [relabeling the old "(E)" to "(F)"]. The new section (E) says: "E. For purposes of this section, there is no coverage for any insured while occupying a motor vehicle owned by, or furnished or available for the regular use of the named insured, a resident spouse of the named insured, or a resident relative of the named insured, if such motor vehicle is not insured by a motor vehicle insurance policy." The Court admitted that Conner's motorcycle was "insured by a motor vehicle insurance policy," which would seem to indicate that 3636(E) would thus have nothing to do with the analysis. However, the Court reasoned: "¶8 Even though Plaintiff did obtain liability insurance on his motorcycle through AIG, because UM coverage is mandatory unless waived, the presumption exists that he also had recourse to some UM benefits. Thus, the policy exclusion which does not allow UM coverage from extending to a vehicle which Defendant does not insure and which is not otherwise covered for UM by any other insurer is not inconsistent with the purpose of §3636(E)."

The Supreme Court later weighed in on the validity of the exclusion in *Morris v America First Ins. Co.* 2010 OK 35, 240 P.3d 661. The Court seemed to find that the validity of the exclusion depended on whether the injured insured had another vehicle with some UM coverage.

Mr. Morris was driving his Freightliner semi truck as a contractor when he was involved in an accident. Understanding the Morris case requires understanding the insurance status of three groups of insured vehicles: 1) Mr. Morris' Freightliner was insured for Liability insurance but had no UM; 2) Mr. Morris owned two other vehicles that were insured by Allstate and they had UM; 3) Mr. Morris was a resident relative of his parent's home, and his parents had UM coverage with America First. Allstate paid its UM limits. America First denied coverage for the accident. They admitted that Mr. Morris was a "resident relative" insured under the policy, but they looked to an exclusion which excluded coverage for "bodily injury sustained by any insured who is a resident family member, while occupying, or when struck by, any motor vehicle owned by that person which is not insured for uninsured motorist coverage at the time of the accident." Since Mr. Morris was occupying a vehicle that had no UM coverage at the time of the accident, America First denied coverage for the accident.

The Supreme Court held that America First's coverage denial was improper. The Court noted that Mr. Morris had UM coverage that protected him while he was driving the Freightliner (the Allstate coverage for his other vehicles) even though it was not UM specifically attached to the Freightliner policy. Since UM coverage follows the person rather than the vehicle, the Court reasoned that America First could not validly rely only on the lack of UM coverage on the Freightliner policy, but must look instead to whether Mr. Morris had UM coverage from any source (the Allstate policy) that covered him while he was driving the Freightliner.

The Court also discussed the *Conner* case, distinguishing it and apparently approving of its holding (¶¶ 13 - 18). The insured in *Conner* had no other UM coverage that he could point to (as Mr. Morris had the Allstate UM coverage) that would apply to his use of the motorcycle. Thus Mr. Conner truly was uninsured for UM and thus, "an insurance company, with the proper exclusion, may preclude UM coverage from extending to such a vehicle." ¶ 17.

§6:49 -The named driver exclusion. [NEW]

The Supreme Court has determined that an auto Liability insurer is entitled to exclude named individuals from coverage by using a "named driver endorsement." See *Pierce v Oklahoma Property and Casualty Ins. Co.*, 1995 OK 78, 901 P.2d 819, discussed at §5:10 in the main volume. The holding in *Pierce* was applied to an Uninsured Motorist provision in *O'Brien v Dorrough*, 1996 OK CIV APP 25, 928 P.2d 322.

In *Alternative Medicine of Tulsa, Inc. v Cates*, 2006 OK CIV APP 65, 136 P.3d 716, the Court of Civil Appeals invalidated a named driver exclusion at least so far as it defeated UM coverage for innocent third parties riding in the vehicle driven by the excluded driver.

§6:55 Limits of Liability.

§6:60 --The Workers Compensation set-off.

In *Wise v. Wollery*, 1995 OK CIV APP 69, 904 P.2d 151, the Workers' Compensation carrier sought apportionment of an employee's recovery from an employer's uninsured motorist coverage in accordance with another provision of 85 O.S. § 44. The Workers' Compensation carrier argued that the public policy reasons expressed in *Bill Hodges Truck Co. v Humphrey*, 1984 OK CIV APP 55, 704 P.2d 94, *cert den.* (1985), do not apply to UM coverage paid for by an employer. In *Wise*, the Court of Appeals held that while § 44 does not ordinarily allow a claimant double recovery, "uninsured motorist benefits constitute an exception to the rule whether such benefits are paid for by the employee or by some other party". Also see *Dennis v Harding Glass Co.*, 1996 OK CIV APP 105, 929 P.2d 301.

§6:65 Validity of provisions that reduce the limits of liability for certain insureds.

In *Gray by and through Gray v Midland Risk Ins. Co.*, 1996 OK 111, 925 P.2d 560, the insured vehicle was owned by Tammy and Gary Robbins. The policy had a provision stating that the limits of liability for bodily injury and property damage would be reduced to the Oklahoma statutory limits of liability for any claim arising from an automobile accident occurring while any automobile was being driven by any driver not listed on the endorsement.

The policy normally provided $50,000 in UM. However, an accident occurred while the vehicle was being driven by someone who was not listed on the "endorsement." The insurer argued that, under the terms of the policy, they were only liable for $10,000 UM coverage, rather than the stated $50,000. The Court held that this language, which reduced the UM coverage to the statutory minimums under certain circumstances, was valid under Oklahoma law.

For an interesting case dealing with the interrelation between UM coverage and workers compensation payments, see *Hartford Ins. Co. v Dyer*, 2002 OK CIV APP 126, 61 P.3d 912 discussed in §6:101. This case does not really deal with the workers compensation "setoff," but anyone who has a case involving both UM and workers compensation should review it.

§6:70 The Other Insurance Clause. "Stacking" of UM coverages, and the "exhaustion" requirement.

§6:71 -In General.

In *Reeder v American Economy Ins. Co.*, 88 F.3d 892 (10th Cir. 1996), the Court discussed the mathematics of "stacking." When coverages are "stacked," they are aggregated so that the coverages are placed "end to end" to form an effectively larger coverage. If there are three "stacked" $500,000 policies, the insured will then effectively have access to $1,500,000 in coverage. However, “stacked” policies are not “collateralized.” If there are $612,000 in damages, the insured will collect her $612,000 out of the $1,500,000 in coverage. If the three policies were “collateralized,” the insured would be entitled to recover her $612,000 in damage by treating each $500,000 coverage as a separate entity, and recovering each $500,000 limit, for a total of $1.5 million. The Court would not allow this type of recovery.

§6.77 -Stacking. Fleet stacking.

For another case refusing to allow fleet stacking, see *Widmann v Acceptance Ins. Co.*, 2002 OK CIV APP 118, 63 P.3d 23.

In *Haberman v The Hartford Ins. Group*, 443 F.3d 1257 (10th Cir., 2006), the named insured on a Hartford commercial policy was a professional corporation. However, Haberman, the owner of the corporation, was listed by name, in a "Named Persons Endorsement." The Endorsement said that it "modifies insurance provided under the...Business Auto Coverage Form" and that Haberman is an "'insured' for Liability Coverage" under the "Liability Coverage" section of the policy. Haberman was involved in an accident in a friend's vehicle and made a UM claim against the Hartford policy. Hartford argued that the Endorsement extended coverage to Haberman individually only under the Liability policy. However, the Tenth Circuit held that the language of the Endorsement plainly extended Haberman coverage under the entire Busienss Auto Coverage or, in the alternative, was at least ambiguous and could be read to extend coverage to Haberman to the entire Business Auto Coverage, which would include UM. The Tenth Circuit further held that, once it was determined that Haberman was a defined named insured under the UM portion of the Hartford policy, Haberman was then entitled to "stack" the UM coverage available on the two vehicles covered under the Hartford polciy. This case is also discussed in §§1:2, 2:2 and 6:32.

The practitioner should also examine 36 O.S. §3637, noted in §6.2, and determine whether the commercial policy in question is even covered under the UM statute.

§6:78 -The Limits of Stacking: The Payment of a Single Premium for coverage of Multiple Vehicles.

The Supreme Court reversed the Court of Civil Appeals decision, *Kinder v Oklahoma Farmers Union Mutual Ins. Co.*, 1991 OK CIV APP 53, 813 P.2d 546. *Kinder I* was remanded to the trial court. After a second judgment, a new appeal ensued. In *Kinder v Oklahoma Farmers Union Mutual Ins. Co.*, 1997 OK 104, 943 P.2d 617 (*Kinder II*), the Supreme Court held, as it did in *Withrow v Pickard*, 1995 OK 120, 905 P.2d 800, "that nothing in our statutes requires an insurer to offer stackable UM coverage in a single insurance policy which covers multiple vehicles. Since the plaintiff had obtained the maximum amount of UM coverage permitted, (i.e., that amount equal to his liability limits), since he had paid only one premium, and since the policy plainly stated that the UM coverage was not based on the number of vehicles, the plaintiff was not entitled to stack his UM coverage." *Kinder II*, at 620.

Also see, *Mid-Continent Group v Henry*, 2003 OK CIV APP 46, 69 P.3d 1216 (discussed in §6:119 supra), where the Court of Civil Appeals held that the addition of a third vehicle to an existing policy covering two vehicles essentially created a "new policy" that required a new offer and rejection of UM. Only one UM premium had been paid under the original two vehicle policy. The Court held that, to avoid stacking (under *Withrow v. Pickard,* 1995 OK 120, 905 P.2d 800) the insurer must show 1) collection of only one premium, and 2) adequate notice to the insured of his "UM options." Since no new offer was made under the new policy, the insured had not been given adequate notice of his UM options and the insurer was obligated to stack the three available UM coverages, despite the fact that only one UM premium was collected.

In *Spears v Glens Falls Ins. Co.*, 2005 OK 35, 114 P.3d 448, the Court held that the insurer was not obligated to provide the insured with pre-policy notice that the insurance policy, covering multiple vehicles, would not "stack." The insured recognized that only one premium was paid and, thus, normally there would be no stacking under *Scott v Cimarron Ins. Co., Inc.*, 1989 OK 26, 774 P.2d 456 and *Withrow v Pickard*, 1995 OK 120, 905 P.2d 800. However, the insured argued that in those cases the insurance carrier had apparently advised the insured, prior to their agreement to purchase the policies, that there would be no stacking. Spears pointed out that Glens Falls Ins. had not given this type of warning to the insured prior to the purchase of the policy in 1993. However, the Supreme Court held that pre-policy notice of "no stacking" was not required. The Supreme Court further held that *Kinder v Oklahoma Farmers Union Mut. Ins. Co*, 1991 OK CIV APP 53, 813 P.2d 546 and *Mid-Continent Group v Henry*, 2003 OK CIV AP 46, 69 P.3d 1216 were overruled to the extent they may have required such pre-policy notice.

§6:79 -Requirement that the tortfeasor's liability insurance be "exhausted by payment" before the UM coverage is payable.

The case of *Hibbs v Farmers Ins. Co., Inc.*, 1985 OK 77, 725 P.2d 1232 has been generally overruled. The reader should examine §6:80 for a discussion of *Mustain v United States Fidelity and Guaranty Co.*, 1996 OK 98, 925 P.2d 533.

§6:80 -Primary UM vs Excess UM. The valid application of the "Other Insurance" provision and of the "exhaustion" requirement.

The Supreme Court has changed what we thought we knew about the "exhaustion" requirement, making the title to this section of the Book misleading. In *Keel v MFA Insurance Company*, 1976 OK 86, 553 P.2d 153 the Court first held that excess clauses could validly be used to determine the order of payment between insurers. In *Hibbs v Farmers Ins. Co., Inc.*, 1985 OK 77, 725 P.2d 1232, the Court held that the excess UM insurer does not have to make payment unless and until the primary UM insurance is exhausted by payment.

This was changed in *Mustain v United States Fidelity and Guaranty Co.*, 1996 OK 98, 925 P.2d 533. The insured was injured while using a crane attached to a truck. The truck was insured for UM by U.S.F.&G. The insured had personal UM insurance through American Employers Ins. Co.. The insured brought suit against both UM insurers, but later settled his action against U.S.F.&G. by accepting payment of only a portion of the available U.S.F.&G. coverage. The insured then sought full recovery against American and the trial court refused.

A reading of *Hibbs* would arguably allow American to go free under these facts, since the primary UM was released without full payment. However, the Supreme Court refused this result, saying:

> Excess provisions in a motor vehicle liability insurance policy are unenforceable if the provisions would allow the insurer to escape liability. In this case, American's reading of the "other insurance" clause would allow it to completely escape liability and thereby defeat the purpose of the controlling statute to protect insured persons who are injured by uninsured/underinsured motorists. *Buzzard v. Farmers Insurance Co.*, 824 P.2d 1105 (Okla.1991), foreshadowed that such escape attempts will be futile and thus altered the consequences of *Hibbs v. Farmers Insurance Co.*, 725 P.2d 1232 (Okla.1985).

The Court then cited the *Buzzard* duty of a UM insurer to evaluate and make an offer of payment even though the underlying Liability insurer had not yet paid. The Court said the same duty applied to an excess UM insurer when the primary UM insurance had not yet been exhausted. "We therefore hold that as between the insurer and its insured UM insurance is primary coverage." *Id.* at 536. The Court reasoned that "subrogation rights" would "guard against one insurer shifting the burden of loss to another or escaping the burden of loss through token settlements." *Id.* If the excess insurer ends up paying first, the trial court should be able to allow recoupment between the insurers. The Court specifically found that "any part of *[Hibbs]* which is inconsistent with the UM insurer's responsibility and liability under § 3636 as construed herein, shall have no further precedential value."

In another case, issued about the same time, *Pentz v Davis*, 1996 OK 86, 927 P.2d 538, the Supreme Court, again discussed the "primary" status of UM coverage. The injured claimant was a passenger in a privately owned vehicle being driven on church business. The potential UM carriers included American Western (covering the vehicle that Pentz was riding in), Church Mutual (a general liability policy issued to the church), Allstate (Pentz's personal UM) and Oklahoma Farm Bureau (Pentz's personal UM). Pentz did not submit a claim against American Western, the insurer of the car that Pentz was riding in. He sued Church Mutual, Allstate and Oklahoma Farm Bureau.

The Supreme Court eventually determined that Church Mutual's policy simply provided no UM at all, so this policy is irrelevant to our discussion. Allstate and Oklahoma Farm Bureau both took the position that they could not be compelled to pay UM because their policies were "excess" coverages in this situation and that Pentz had not recovered from the "primary" UM insurer, American Western. This, of course, would be the apparent proper result under *Hibbs v Farmers Insurance Co.*, 1985 OK 77, 725 P.2d 1232.

As it did in *Mustain*, the Court refused to allow the "excess" language in an "other insurance" clause to allow a UM insurer to escape its obligations to its insured. The Court held that, although an "other insurance" clause may well control the rights between the insurers, it does not control the insurer's obligations to its insured.

§6:94 –Keel v MFA and the four alternatives.

The question of "bad faith" is beyond the scope of this book. However, counsel for insurer and insured should be aware of the teachings of *Brown v Patel*, 2007 OK 16, 157 P.3d 117. Brown is a bad faith case, but it also touches on the question of when a UM insurer should properly be allowed to intervene to protect its subrogation rights. The UM insurer in Brown was granted permission by the trial court to intervene in the insured's suit against the tortfeasor. The insured alleged that the intervention, under the circumstances, was bad faith because, among other things, the insurer did not have matured subrogation rights (it had not paid the UM claim at the time of the intervention). The Supreme Court generally reaffirmed the UM insurer's right to intervene. However, it also noted that under 12 O.S. §2024 the "right" to intervene could be as a matter of right (§2024(A)) or permissive (§2024(B)). In general, if an insurer has already paid the UM claim, it can intervene, as a matter of right, to protect its accrued subrogation rights. However, if the insurer has not yet paid the UM claim (such as when it denies coverage, or believes the amount of damages do not justify UM recovery), intervention is not a matter of right, but is permissive. The court may grant the intervention in order to allow the UM insurer to monitor the litigation to make sure the tortfeasor is actively contesting questions of liability and damages. However, even if the court grants intervention, the court can impose restrictions on the UM insurer's right to participate in the litigation.

Any insurer who wishes to intervene in litigation between its insured and the tortfesor should closely examine the *Brown* case. If intervention is sought, insured's counsel should consider whether to object under *Brown*. The case raises a myriad of tactical and "bad faith" concerns that could be a trap for the insurer. Under *Brown* the "right to intervene" is not as certain or automatic as it once was.

§6:96 –The UM insurer's obligation to evaluate the claim and make reasonable settlement offers.

Although "bad faith" claims are outside the scope of this work, it is necessary to discuss some issues that are "bad faith" related because they go to the heart of the insurer's contract obligations. One such obligation under Oklahoma law is the insurer's obligation to make a swift evaluation of the claim and offer payment to the insured, if the situation warrants. See *Buzzard v Farmers Ins. Co.,* 1991 OK 127, 824 P.2d 1105:

> ¶30 If the claim exceeds the amount available under the liability policy, the

> underinsurer must take prompt action to determine what payment is due and may not delay the payment of benefits until exhaustion of liability limits. The underinsurer may not safely await settlement between the liability insurer and the insured. Instead, the insurer must go about the business of investigating and evaluating the claim. An insurer is readily equipped to make such a determination, and to assign a dollar value to the claim. Once this is accomplished, if the insurer determines that the claim does not exceed liability limits, and such valuation is supported by reasonable evidence, the underinsurer may delay payment. However, if the underinsurer does not conduct an investigation, or after investigation, determines that the likely worth of the claim exceeds the liability limits, prompt payment must be offered.

In *Newport v USAA*, 2000 OK 59, 11 P.3d 190, the Court held that an insurer who makes "low ball" offers of settlement to the insured (offers below the value assigned to the claim by the insurer), could potentially be liable to the insured for bad faith. The Court explained the result by reference to *Buzzard*:

> ¶ 16 This Court holds that following "an investigation reasonably appropriate under the circumstances," *Buzzard II*, 824 P.2d at 1109, an insurer must promptly settle the

> claim for the value or within the range of value assigned to the claim as a result of its investigation. An insurer's failure to do so may subject it to a claim for bad faith from its insured. This is not to say an insurer may not negotiate or litigate the value of the claim. The duty of good faith and fair dealing merely prevents an insurer from offering less than what its own investigation reveals to be the claim's value.
>
> ¶ 17 The Court of Civil Appeals in this matter held that there was no bad faith because the claim was not actually denied and negotiations were ongoing. However, an offer to make an insufficient payment is equivalent to a denial of that portion of the claim lying between the insurer's offer and the value or range of value which the insurer has assigned to the claim. Offers below the insurer's own calculation of the value of the claim are not a valid justification for withholding payment.

However, in a footnote, the Court also noted that, "Not every cause in which an insurer offers to settle a claim at a value less than that at which it originally evaluated a loss will support an award of bad faith damages. Under the facts presented--where the insurer's original offer was $250,000 less than the lowest value estimated for the claim, where offers were tendered which were difficult to appraise at a current value, and where the final offer [the first one which fell within the appraised value of the claim] was accompanied by a threat that the insured might come away with nothing at trial--bad faith damages are recoverable."

§6:100 Subrogation and the Trust Agreement.

§6:101 -In General.

For a lawsuit that was more equivalent to a law school exam question (which this writer had some hand in at the early stages) see *Hartford Ins. Co. v Dyer*, 2002 OK CIV APP 126, 61 P.3d 912. In 1988, Assalone brought an action against her UM carrier, Hartford. She also recovered workers compensation benefits from Travelers. Assalone did not bring a claim against Dyer, the tortfeasor, but Travelers did bring a subrogation suit against Dyer. Hartford then brought a subrogation third party action against Dyer in the Assalone v Hartford case. The actions were consolidated and Assalone amended to claim bad faith against Hartford. Hartford claimed that its subrogation rights had been impaired by Assalone's failure to join Dyer as a party. Dyer claimed that Hartford had no mature subrogation rights because Hartford had not yet paid Assalone's claim. Hartford and Dyer were both granted summary judgment and the issues went up on appeal. See the discussion of *Assalone v. Hartford Acc. & Indem. Co.*, 1994 OK CIV APP 64, 908 P.2d 812 in the original volume, §6:106. While the appeal was pending, Dyer and Travelers settled the workers compensation subrogation claim, with a full release.

In the *Assalone v Hartford* appeal, the Court of Civil Appeals held that Assalone was not required to take affirmative acts (sue Dyer) to preserve Hartford's subrogation rights against Dyer. The case was remanded. Hartford and Assalone ultimately settled Assalone's UM claim, leaving alive only the *Hartford v Dyer* subrogation claim. At the *Hartford v Dyer* trial, the court refused to allow Hartford to introduce any medical bills that Dyer had already paid in the settlement of the *Travelers v Dyer* workers compensation subrogation action. The *Hartford v Dyer* jury returned a verdict for $15,000. The trial court further reduced this verdict by the $15,000.50 that Dyer had previously paid to Travelers for workers compensation PPD, leaving a verdict of zero for Hartford.

The Court of Civil Appeals held that the trial court acted properly in not allowing Hartford to introduce evidence of medical bills that had been recovered by Travelers in the workers compensation subrogation settlement. Travelers was subrogated to those medical bills, and Dyer had already paid those amounts. Hartford was subrogated only to the amounts that it had paid under UM. Because Dyer had previously paid, and been released from, the medical bills paid by Travelers, Hartford could not even recover them as a "trustee" for Travelers.

However, the Court held that Dyer was not

entitled to reduce the Hartford judgment by the amount of PPD payments Dyer had previously paid to Travelers. Although PPD may, in some sense, represent some of the same "disability" amounts (pain and suffering and lost wages) that Hartford was recovering for in its current $15,000 judgment, the Court held that PPD was a statutory creature and that Dyer could not reduce the *Hartford v Dyer* judgment by the amount of PPD paid to Travelers.

On a cross appeal, Dyer argued that Hartford was not entitled to recover any amounts, because Hartford had not proven that it had paid a valid UM claim. Dyer's Liability Insurance limits were $100,000. The jury had found that Assalone's claim was worth $15,000 (without seeing the $16,510.12 in medical benefits paid by Travelers). Had Hartford proven that the value of Assalone's claim exceeded Dyer's Liability limits? The Court of Civil Appeals held that this did not matter. Hartford had paid certain amounts under a UM claim. Under *Burch v. Allstate Ins. Co.*, 1998 OK 129, 977 P.2d 1057, Assalone was entitled to collect her full damages from Hartford, leaving Hartford to subrogate against Dyer. Note: the Court does not mention that, arguably, *Burch* only requires a UM carrier to pay the claimant's full claim <u>if</u> the value of the claim exceeds the tortfeasor's Liability limits. In other words, even under *Burch*, Hartford would not have been obligated to pay Assalone's full claim unless the value of Assalone's claim exceeded $100,000. In this writer's opinion, what Dyer was really saying was that

Hartford's UM payment was made as a "volunteer" (since the claim was not worth more than Assalone's $100,000 Liability limits and was thus not a valid UM claim). In ruling in this manner, the Court may simply be saying that it refuses to label a UM carrier like Hartford as a "volunteer" (thus destroying Hartford's subrogation rights) simply because it has wrongly guessed, and paid, the value of it's insured's personal injury claim.

§6:102 - The destruction of subrogation rights by the insured's settlement with the tortfeasor. The "Porter Doctrine."

Phillips v New Hampshire Ins. Co., 263 F.3d 1215 (10th Cir. 2001). Plaintiff employee was injured while driving her personal vehicle on employer's business. Employer had a commercial auto policy with NHIC. Plaintiff filed a workers compensation action against employer and, in discovery, demanded information as to any auto insurance policies that would provide UM for the accident. The employer did not respond until after employee had settled her workers compensation claim, and after employee had settled for the policy limits of the tortfeasor's Liability insurer. When employee finally learned of the existence of the NHIC policy, she demanded payment and NHIC denied the claim, arguing that the NHIC policy did not cover for accidents occurring in the employee's personal vehicle. NHIC also argued that employee had waived her right to claim against the NHIC policy because employee had settled with the tortfeasor without giving notice to NHIC. The District Court agreed with NHIC, and the case went to the Tenth Circuit on appeal.

The Porter Doctrine. Knowing and voluntary waiver. The Tenth Circuit first examined the question in light of Porter v MFA Ins. Co., 1982 OK 23, 643 P.2d 302. The Court noted that in Porter the insured knew of the existence of the UM coverage and knowingly took actions that destroyed the UM insurer's subrogation rights. The Court held that there was no such evidence in this case because the employee did not know of the existence of the UM coverage at the time she released the tortfeasor. Thus, there could not have been a "knowing waiver" of the UM coverage.

Actual prejudice. The Tenth Circuit held that Oklahoma law would also require the UM insurer to establish "actual prejudice" from the employee's destruction of NHIC's subrogation rights. Obviously referring to the fact that the tortfeasor may have been "judgment proof," the Court held that NHIC had not established "actual prejudice" so as to be entitled to summary judgment on this issue. Thus, it appears that the Tenth Circuit would require the insurer show "actual prejudice" by the release of the tortfeasor, and that the UM insurer could not complain about the loss of subrogation rights against a judgment proof tortfeasor.

Estoppel by denying contract. The Court noted that NHIC had denied that NHIC owed the employee UM coverage in the first place. Citing a line of Oklahoma Supreme Court cases, the Court held that an insurer who denies the existence of a UM contract can not complain over a violation of that contract if the claimant settles with the tortfeasor. The Court held that it made no difference that NHIC's denial of coverage came after the employee had already destroyed NHIC's subrogation rights.

Business insurer's obligation to notify employees of potential rights under policy. The Court held that a business insurer, like NHIC, had an obligation to notify potential insureds (such as the employee here) of their right to make claim under the business UM policy, at least if the business insurer expected to require the employee to protect the insurer's subrogation rights under the contract.

> The UM/UIM insurer must take prompt action to determine what payment is due if the insured's damages exceed the liability coverage available under the tort-feasor's policy. See *Buzzard*, 824 P.2d at 1112. Thus, in commercial/business policies that cover employees, the UM/UIM insurer may also have a concomitant duty to inform an injured employee-insured who may be ignorant of

potential coverage and contract terms of its right to contractual or statutory subrogation if the insurer wishes to later elect to exercise that right. See *Uptegraft*, 662 P.2d at 687 n. 11 (citing New Jersey case holding that if an insurance contract has a cooperation agreement, "the initial responsibility to act to protect subrogated rights rests upon the insurer.... [W]hen an insurer sits on these rights, it cannot be heard to complain."); *Sexton*, 816 P.2d at 1138 (noting the insurer's duty to "aid its insured in the preservation of its subrogation rights") (quotation omitted). At the very least, the insurer has a duty to promptly produce a policy on request to an injured employee with a colorable claim under the policy so that the employee may ascertain whether he is covered and what responsibilities he has under the contract.

Id. at 1224.

The "substitute payment" provisions of §3636(E). The Court also dealt with the applicability of the "substitute payment" notice provisions set forth in §3636(E). Obviously plaintiff employee had failed to give proper "notice" of intent to settle under §3636(E). The Tenth Circuit noted that §3636(E) provided a method for the UM insurer to retain its subrogation rights, while still providing the UM insured with the benefit of an early payment (albeit, from the UM insurer rather than from the tortfeasor's

Liability insurer). However, "the only time taking such action would be profitable to the UM/UIM carrier is when the tort-feasor has assets beyond the liability limits (or settlement offer) of his insurance policy that may be collected after judgment."

The Tenth Circuit was also of the opinion that an insured's failure to comply with §3636(E) was not necessarily fatal to the insured's UM claim. §3636(E) provides the insured with a mechanism for getting early payment of the tortfeasor's Liability money. However, this Court finds that an insured's failure to follow §3636(E) does not destroy the insured's right to collect from the UM insurer, at least under these facts.

§6:105 - Protection of subrogation rights using the "substitute payment" provisions of §3636(E). What happens when the tortfeasor's liability insurer offers to pay liability limits.

The *Barnes* case, Barnes *v Oklahoma Farm Bureau* 1998 OK CIV APP 168, 869 P.2d 852 (*Barnes I*), discussed in the main volume, confirmed that a "substitute payment" under 36 O.S. §3636(E) was not a payment of UM policy proceeds, but was merely the cost the UM insurer must pay if it wants to retain its' subrogation rights after the Liability insurer offers to pay its policy limits. *Barnes I* went back to the trial court for a trial of the still-pending "bad faith" claim against the UM insurer. The insured claimed that the insurer was in bad faith because it had offered to make a "substitute payment" after the Liability insurer offered its' limits, but, as part of that offer, had demanded that the insured sign a Partial Release acknowledging that the substitute payment would reduce the insurer's ultimate UM obligation. The UM insurer defended by claiming that it had reasonably relied upon a legal opinion by outside counsel in demanding the Partial Release. After a bad faith judgment was rendered against the insurer, the Supreme Court got the case on appeal. *Barnes v Oklahoma Farm Bureau Mut. Ins.*, 2000 OK 55, 11 P.3d 162. Among other issues, the Court discussed whether the insurer had a reasonable basis to rely upon the legal opinion. The Supreme Court held that the concept of the "substitute payment" was so easy to grasp, and it was so obvious that the legal opinion was wrong, that the insurer could not have reasonably relied upon it. The Supreme Court said:

> ¶ 28 To protect its subrogation right(s) once notified of a tentative liability limits settlement, a UIM carrier must "substitute its payment to the insured for the tentative settlement amount" and "then [it will] be entitled to the insured's right of recovery to the extent of such payment and any settlement under the [UIM] coverage." § 3636(E)(2)(emphasis added). If no substitution is made the UIM "insurer has no right to the proceeds of any settlement or judgment, as provided herein, for any amount

paid under the [UIM] coverage." § 3636(E)(2).

¶ 29 It is unmistakable from reading § 3636(E)(2) that a substituted payment for the tentative settlement being offered by Donaldson could not conceivably also be considered as a payment under the UIM coverage, the position taken by insurer. It is also unmistakable that a substitution for a tentative liability limits settlement offer, in order to protect the UIM carrier's subrogation rights, does not relieve the UIM carrier of its responsibility to pay to its insured the full amount of underinsurance coverage when a reasonable evaluation of the insured's injuries/damages equal or exceed the limits of both the tortfeasor's liability coverage and the UIM coverage. As the COCA correctly noted in Barnes I, "[a]lthough [insurer's] 'exposure' in this case is $25,000 if it had properly substituted Donaldson's [tentative] settlement, insurer would have been subrogated to Barnes' right to $10,000 and would only pay out the amount that it had contracted with Barnes to provide [,]" i.e. $15,000--the latter amount also subject to potential recoupment by the UIM insurer from any available assets of the tortfeasor.

In 2004 36 O.S. § 3636(E) was redesignated as (F).

In *Gregg v Le Mars Ins. Co.*, 2009 OK CIV APP 93, 227 P.3d 1107, the Court held that if a UM carrier waives subrogation under § 3636(F), the carrier has not made an admission of coverage under its UM policy.

§6:106 -Subrogation and the Statute of Limitations problem.

The case of *Burch v Allstate Ins. Co.*, 1998 OK 129, 977 P.2d 1057 may have some bearing on the statute of limitations problem. Some readers of *Burch* may take the position that the tortfeasor's Liability insurance becomes "unavailable" after the statute of limitations runs against the tortfeasor. This writer does not believe that this is a proper reading of *Burch*, however, this will likely be a matter of controversy. See the discussion on this point in §6.36 above.

However, that decidedly was the holding in *Kavanaugh v Maryland Insurance Co., Inc.*, 1997 OK CIV APP 41, 943 P.2d 629. The *Kavanaugh* case is a good example of the strategic maneuvering that may become common under *Burch* if *Burch* is construed to say that the running of the tort statute of limitations makes the Liability insurance "unavailable." Once again, we will let the *Burch* Court describe the *Kavanaugh* case:

> [T]he injured party brought suit against the

> tortfeasor within the limitations period, but dismissed the suit without prejudice approximately three years later. After dismissing her suit against the tortfeasor, the insured sued her UM carrier, seeking recovery of her total damages. The insurer interposed *Buzzard.* The insured argued that *Buzzard* applied only where the tortfeasor's insurance remains available. Since the tortfeasor's liability insurance was no longer available to her, *Buzzard* was inapplicable. Relying on our decisions in *Bohannan v. Allstate Insurance Co.* and *Uptegraft v. Home Insurance Co.*, the appellate court held that the insurer should be liable for the *entire* damages claimed by the insured if the tortfeasor's liability insurance is no longer available as long as the insured did nothing affirmatively to cause the liability insurance to become unavailable.

The *Burch* Court obviously would agree with the result in *Kavanaugh*. The Liability insurance was insufficient to pay for the claim; therefore there it was a UM claim. However, the *Burch* Court disagreed with the underlying logic of the *Kavanaugh* case. The *Kavanaugh* case held that, once the case against the tortfeasor was dismissed, and the statute of limitations ran, the tortfeasor's Liability limits were no longer "available." However, the "availability" argument is unnecessary under *Burch.* The Liability insurance was insufficient to pay for the claimant's entire damages and that alone is enough to require the UM insurer to pay the entire loss under *Burch*.

This writer believes that this question was put to rest in the Court's decision in *Gates v Eller*, 2001 OK 38, 22 P.3d 1215 (discussed fully in §6:36 above). There the Court held that the tortfeasor's Liability insurance did not become "unavailable" simply because the claimant allowed the statute of limitations to run against the tortfeasor. That means that, if the value of the claimant's claim is less than the tortfeasor's Liability insurance, there is no UM claim because the tortfeasor is not an "uninsured motorist." That result is not changed when the statute of limitations runs against the tortfeasor.

The case of *Farmers Ins. Co., Inc. v Estate of Stark*, 1996 OK CIV APP 53, 924 P.2d 798 held that a UM carrier's subrogation action against tortfeasor to recoup the UM carrier's payment was untimely when not brought within the two years that the insured had after her accident to sue tortfeasor, which ran from date of insured's accident. The theory of the *Stark* case was upheld by the Supreme Court in *Employers Mut. Cas. Co. v. Mosby*, 1997 OK 93, 943 P.2d 593, which held that a UM carrier's subrogation claim was time-barred when it was not brought within two years of the date of accident. The subrogee steps into the shoes of its claimant and takes the claim subject to defenses based on the date of accrual to the claimant.

Also, see *Phillips v New Hampshire Ins. Co.*, 263 F.3d 1215 (10th Cir. 2001) discussed in §6:102 above.

§6:115 The Creation of the Contract. Mandatory Offer, Rejection, and Related Issues.

§6:119 -The unmade offer and the bad rejection.

The Supreme Court has specifically held that the "implied" UM coverage, written into a policy when there was no UM rejection, or a faulty UM rejection, will be at the statutory minimum amounts. In *May v National Union Fire Ins. Co.*, 1996 OK 52, 918 P.2d 43, the Court held that if an insurer failed to offer in writing, or obtain a valid UM rejection form, the amount of UM implied would be the statutory minimum, (at that time, $10,000/20,000), rather than the maximum amount of the available Liability insurance. The Tenth Circuit applied this decision in *May v National Union Fire Ins. Co.*, 84 F.3d 1342 (10th Cir. 1996). For a similar decision, see *Boerstler v Hoover*, 1997 OK 106, 943 P.2d 614.

Also see, *Mid-Continent Group v Henry*, 2003 OK CIV APP 46, 69 P.3d 1216. The insured had a preexisting policy covering two vehicles. This was a non-stackable policy where the insurer collected only one premium for UM coverage. The insured added a third vehicle and the insurer neglected to get a UM waiver when the third vehicle was added. The Court of Civil Appeals held:

1) Under *Beauchamp v. Southwestern National Insurance Company,* 1987 OK 111, ¶ 10, 746 P.2d 673, 676, the addition of a third vehicle to the policy created an entirely "new policy and not a renewal."

2) Since this was a "new policy," the insurer was obligated to provide the insured with a new informed opportunity to waive or reject UM coverage on all three vehicles.

3) Failure to provide this opportunity (failure to obtain a new rejection form as to all three vehicles) meant that UM coverage would be "implied" for all three vehicles.

4) Under *Withrow v. Pickard,* 1995 OK 120, 905 P.2d 800, the insurer can avoid stacking if a) only one UM premium is paid for the entire policy, and b) the insured is given notice of his "UM options" so that he can make an informed decision whether he wants a non-stackable policy. Since the insured was given no such "notice" under the new policy, then the Court held that all three "implied" UM coverages under the new policy would stack. The insured was entitled to collect $30,000 rather than $10,000.

In *Spears v Glens Falls Ins. Co.*, 2005 OK 35, 114 P.3d 448, the Court held that pre-policy notice of "no stacking" was not required. The Supreme Court further held that *Kinder v Oklahoma Farmers Union Mut. Ins. Co,* 1991 OK CIV APP 53, 813 P.2d 546 and *Mid-Continent Group v Henry*, 2003 OK CIV AP

46, 69 P.3d 1216 were overruled to the extent they may have required such pre-policy notice.

§6:121 -When is a new offer or rejection necessary?

Also see, *Mid-Continent Group v Henry*, 2003 OK CIV APP 46, 69 P.3d 1216 (discussed in §6:119 supra), where the Court of Civil Appeals held that the addition of a third vehicle to an existing policy covering two vehicles essentially created a "new policy" that required a new offer and rejection of UM.

The "right to reject" has been moved to §(G) of 36 O.S. §3636. Also, as of November 1, 2009, the Oklahoma Legislature amended this section to do away with the requirement that the insurance agent obtain a new signed rejection form after various changes are made to a policy. Under the 2009 amendment, the company need not obtain any new rejection form. The section now reads:

> G. A named insured or applicant shall have the right to reject uninsured motorist coverage in writing. The form signed by the insured or applicant which initially rejects coverage or selects lower limits shall remain valid for the life of the policy and the completion of a new selection form shall not be required when a renewal, reinstatement, substitute,

replacement, or amended policy is issued to the same-named insured by the same insurer or any of its affiliates. Any changes to an existing policy, regardless of whether these changes create new coverage, do not create a new policy and do not require the completion of a new form.

After selection of limits, rejection, or exercise of the option not to purchase uninsured motorist coverage by a named insured or applicant for insurance, the insurer shall not be required to notify any insured in any renewal, reinstatement, substitute, amended or replacement policy as to the availability of such uninsured motorist coverage or such optional limits. Such selection, rejection, or exercise of the option not to purchase uninsured motorist coverage by a named insured or an applicant shall be valid for all insureds under the policy and shall continue until a named insured requests in writing that the uninsured motorist coverage be added to an existing or future policy of insurance.

§6:122 -Who must sign the rejection form?

The question of whether an "agent" can purport to sign a UM waiver came up again in *Traders Ins. Co. v Johnson*, 2010 OK CIV APP 37, 231 P.3d 790. The Johnsons, husband and wife, purchased their Traders Insurance policy in 2006 through a local insurance agent, Aballtime. Both husband and wife signed the UM waiver form. In 2008, the Johnsons sent their daughter to take a premium payment to Aballtime. She had also been instructed by her parents to have Aballtime issue a new Traders policy for an additional vehicle. Aballtime asked the daughter to sign the policy for the parents and to also sign the UM waiver. About a month later there was an accident and the mother argued that the UM waiver on the additional vehicle was not valid (since it had not been signed by Mr. or Mrs. Johnson). The Court of Civil Appeals held that it was a question of fact as to whether the daughter had been given implied authority to act as the agent of the parents to sign the policy application and UM waiver. "We find nothing in the statutory language that prohibits an agent with actual or apparent authority from rejecting UM coverage on behalf of his or her principal." Id. at ¶14.

§6:131 -Choice of Law.

Choice of law issues were discussed in *Leader National Ins. v Shaw*, 901 F.Supp. 316 (W.D.Ok. 1995). A UM policy was issued in Kansas to Kansas residents. However, the accident occurred in Oklahoma, where insured was domiciled, car involved in accident was financed through Oklahoma dealer, and majority of claimants were residents of Oklahoma. The Court used the "greater contacts" portion of the *Bohannan* analysis and held that Oklahoma had a much greater interest in policy proceeds being sought by Oklahoma residents so that Oklahoma law would apply.

Also see, *Herren v Farm Bureau Mutual Ins. Co., Inc.*, 2001 OK CIV APP 82, 26 P.3d 120. Plaintiffs were involved in an accident that occurred in Oklahoma. They made claims against UM policies that were issued when one insured was a resident of Missouri and another was a resident of Kansas. Before these two policies were scheduled for renewal, the insureds moved to Oklahoma. Based on the law of the states where the policies were issued, neither policy would provide coverage because the tortfeasor's Liability coverage exceeded the amount of the UM (a calculation that is irrelevant under Oklahoma UM law). The insureds argued that it would violate Oklahoma public policy to apply the law of the states where the policies were issued. Looking to *Bohannan v. Allstate Ins. Co.*, 1991 OK 64, 820 P.2d 787, the Court of Civil Appeals noted that there were no Oklahoma UM policies involved in the case at bar and that application of the law of the place of contract (Kansas and Missouri) would thus not offend any Oklahoma public policy governing Oklahoma UM policies. The Court agreed with the trial court that the Court should apply the laws of the state where the UM policies were entered into, rather than Oklahoma UM law. The Court rejected the argument that Oklahoma law should apply simply because the insured vehicles were now garaged in Oklahoma (the policies were issued in Kansas and Missouri, and there had been no renewal of the policies since moving to Oklahoma).

The applicability of out-of-state UM laws came up again in *Burgess v State Farm Mut. Auto. Ins. Co.*, 2003 OK 85, 77 P.3d 612. Burgess was a passenger in his daughter's car and was injured by the negligence of another vehicle driven by Lepley. His daughter and Lepley were Oklahoma residents. Burgess was a Kansas resident. Lepley's $100,000 Liability policy paid, as did his daughter's $10,000 UM policy. Burgess was also insured by State Farm under two $100,000 UM policies covering his vehicles back in Kansas. Kansas law provided that the two $100,000 policies did not "stack," and also provided that the UM coverage could be reduced by the amount of the tortfeasor's Liability coverage. State Farm took the position that, with no stacking, there was only $100,000 UM available, and it was completely "set-off" by the $100,000 paid by Lepley's Liability coverage, so that nothing was due under the Kansas UM policies. Burgess conceded that, under *Bohanan v Allstate Ins. Co.*, 1991 OK 64, 820 P.2d 787, the Oklahoma court should give credence to the Kansas "set-off" provision. However, Burgess argued that, under *Bohanan*, that the Kansas no-stacking rule violated Oklahoma public policy and should not be enforced. The Court of Civil Appeals disagreed, noting that, in *Bohanan*, enforcement of the out-of-state UM rules were not enforced because to do so would cause an effective loss of UM coverage under an Oklahoma policy, which was against Oklahoma public policy. However, in Burgess, the Oklahoma UM policy had been fully paid and was not affected by the Kansas policy or Kansas law.

In *Bernal v Charter County Mut. Ins. Co.*, 2009 OK 28, 209 P.3d 309, the insured vehicle was registered and principally garaged in Texas and the Charter policy was issued in Texas. Billy, an Oklahoma resident, was a passenger in the insured vehicle, driven by Brandon when it had an accident that killed Billy. The accident was caused by Brandon's negligence. An Oklahoma policy insuring Billy paid its UM coverage. Charter, the Texas insurer, paid its liability coverage but refused to pay UM because of a policy provision, valid under Texas law, that would exclude the covered vehicle (the car being driven by Brandon) from the definition of "uninsured motor vehicle." Plaintiff argued that Oklahoma law (which would have invalidated such a policy limitation) should apply. Under *Bohanan v Allstate Ins. Co.*, 1991 OK 64, 820 P.2d 787, Oklahoma courts should apply Oklahoma's choice of law rule to this contract case, which "provides the validity, interpretation, application and effect of the provisions of a motor vehicle insurance contract should be determined in accordance with the laws of the state in which the contract was made, unless (1) those provisions are contrary to Oklahoma's public policy or (2) the facts demonstrate another jurisdiction has the most significant relationship with the subject matter and the parties." *Bernal* at ¶6. However, the Court held that under these facts it did not need to look to the choice of law rule set forth in *Bohanan*, but instead could solve the problem by looking to the Oklahoma statute. The Court noted that 36 O.S. §3636 simply does not purport to control this Texas vehicle. "By its own terms, § 3636(A) applies solely to a policy "issued, delivered, renewed, or extended in this state with respect to a motor vehicle registered or principally garaged in this state . . . ." Since the vehicle was registered in and principally garaged in Texas, the "public policy" embedded in the Oklahoma statute simply did not reach that vehicle and Texas law was free to control the insurance policy. "By legislative force, the terms of § 3636 do not reach all insurance contracts enforceable within the state. Its provisions are inapplicable to a policy issued in Texas that insures a vehicle registered and principally garaged in that state." ¶18. The Court also noted that the existing Oklahoma UM policy (Billy's Oklahoma policy) paid in full and no one was arguing that the existence of the Texas policy had any effect on the payment of the Oklahoma policy. This differentiated the *Beranl* case from the *Bohanan* case.

§6:132 -Hospital and Physician's Liens.

§6:132

According to the Court of Civil Appeals, a trial court can force a Plaintiff's attorney to take his attorneys fees out of the UM recovery in order to allow lien holders to concentrate on the Liability insurance. In *Fugate v Mooney*, 1998 OK CIV APP 48, 958 P.2d 818, the insured had a claim against a tortfeasor and a UM carrier. There was $25,000 in Liability insurance available and $35,000 in UM available. There were also medical bills totaling $180,000, some of which were backed up with filed physician's and hospital liens. Plaintiff's attorney also claimed a 35% attorneys fee lien (apparently $21,000). The Plaintiff asked the trial court to apportion the policy limits settlement.

The trial court found that 1) the medical liens did no attach to the insured's UM claim, but 2) under the doctrine of "marshaling of assets," the medical liens would be ordered satisfied out of the $35,000 Liability coverage, and the senior attorneys fee lien of $21,000 would be ordered satisfied out of the $35,000 of UM insurance money (leaving the UM insured with only $14,000 out of the UM money) and 3) various unsecured creditors would be satisfied out of the remaining Liability money.

The insured's attorney argued that he should be able to deduct his attorneys fee pro-rata out of both the Liability and the UM funds, and that the lien claimants should then be required to take what was left of the Liability money. This would leave the UM insured with a larger share of the UM fund, since the attorneys fee would be partially satisfied out of the

Liability money.

However, the Court of Civil Appeals agreed with the trial court on most issues. They found that the doctrine of marshaling of assets applied, and that the senior lien holder (the attorneys lien), did not have to be satisfied on a pro-rata basis out of the Liability and the UM money, but could be ordered satisfied out of the UM fund only.

> Fugate relies on *Vinzant v. Hillcrest Medical Center* (*Vinzant*), 1980 OK 50, 609 P.2d 1274, for the proposition he is entitled to deduct his attorney's fee from a specific check when the total of the attorney's lien and the hospital lien exceeds the liability settlement proceeds. However, in *State ex rel. Dept. of Human Services v. Allstate Ins. Co.,* 1987 OK 91, 744 P.2d 186, 188, the Court clarified *Vinzant*, stating the case does not impose a duty of pro rata payment of attorney fees on lienholders. An attorney's lien is a senior lien that attaches to the entire settlement, not to individual checks in payment of the settlement. Once sufficient settlement funds have been collected to pay the attorney's fee in full, the lien is extinguished. *Id.* at 189.
>
> *Fugate* at 819.

"Under the doctrine of marshaling, a senior lienholder must satisfy its claim by first resorting to the fund in which junior lienholders have no interest.

Martin, In re, 1994 OK 48, 875 P.2d 417, 420, and 24 O.S.1991 § 4." *Id.* at 819. The Court of Civil Appeals did hold, however, that the trial court was in error in allowing unsecured creditors to make claim against the Liability money. This violated the injured claimant's $50,000 exemption from execution for personal injury claims found in 31 O.S.1991 § 1(A)(21).

The Supreme Court has answered the question of whether a physician's lien under 42 O.S. §46 can attach to a patient's right to recover against a UM policy. The Court answered in the affirmative in *Broadway Clinic v Liberty Mut. Ins. Co.*, 2006 OK 29, 139 P.3d 873.

In *PTS Healthcare, Inc. v Mid-Century Ins. Co.*, 2007 OK CIV APP 100, 171 P.3d 924, the Court of Civil Appeals found that physical therapists were not entitled to file liens under 42 O.S. ¶ 46 because a physical therapist was not a "physican" as that term is used in ¶ 46.

However, 42 O.S. ¶ 46 was amended, effective November 1, 2008, to extend the right to file a lien to "any other professional person who engages in the healing arts, within their scope of practice pursuant to Title 59 of the Oklahoma Statutes." Since the Physical Therapy Practice Act is found at 59 O.S. ¶ 887.1, presumably physical therapists are now entitled to file such liens and enforce them against UM recoveries.

§6:133 -Subrogation by other insurers against their insured's Uninsured Motorist recovery.

A workers' compensation insurer is not entitled to subrogate against an injured employee's right of recovery against an Uninsured Motorist insurer. In *Thrasher v Act-Fast Labor Pool, Inc.*, 1991 OK 12, 806 P.2d 640, the employee was riding in a car when it was involved in an accident. Employee filed a workers' compensation claim. Employee then recovered from her co-employee's uninsured motorist insurance, which covered the vehicle that Employee was riding in. The Court held that the workers' compensation insurer did not have subrogation rights against the uninsured motorist benefits.

Similarly, see *Wise v Woolery*, 1995 OK CIV APP 69, 904 P.2d 151. The workers' compensation insurer argued that *Thrasher* should not apply in a situation where the uninsured motorist benefits were paid out of a policy owned by the employer. The Court of Appeals denied subrogation to the workers' compensation insurer. "While [42 O.S.§ 44] ordinarily does not allow double recovery, uninsured motorist benefits constitute an exception to the rule whether such benefits are paid for by the employee or by some other party." *Id.* at 152.

Health insurers and the "make whole" rule and

the "common fund" doctrine.

In *Reeds v Walker*, 2006 OK 43, 157 P.3d 100, the Court held that a health insurer, covered by ERISA, could be subrogated against its insured's right to recover UM benefits. The health insurer's subrogation/reimbursement provision allowed it to recover monies received by the insured by a "third party." The Court held that the UM insurer, in this context, was such a "third party" so that the health insurer would be entitled to reimbursement out of the insured's UM recovery. However, the Court also held that because the insured had not been "made whole" by the UM recovery (see *Equity Fire and Casualty Company v. Youngblood*, 1996 OK 123, 927 P.2d 572), the health insurer could not enforce its reimbursement rights.

Counsel should use caution when dealing with the subrogation/reimbursement rights of any insurer, especially an insurer or plan covered under ERISA. The policy or plan can contain strict language requiring the plan to be reimbursed at 100% out of any recoveries (before payment of any attorneys fees or expenses). Counsel faced with such a reimbursement question should examine *Reed* (and *Youngblood*) closely to determine whether the facts of their case, and the language of the reimbursement provision, would require the insured to reimburse the health insurer out of UM monies. Plumbing the depths of these cases is beyond the scope of this work, but for further discussion of the "make whole" rule, the "common fund" doctrine and ERISA subrogtion/reimbursement rules, see *Equity Fire and Cas Co. v Youngblood*, 1996 OK 123, 927 P.2d 572, *Manokoune v State Farm Mut. Auto. Ins. Co.*, 2006 OK 74, 145 P.3d 1081, *Sollars v Healthcare Recoveries,* 2006 OK CIV APP 140, 140 P.3d 289 and *Reeds v Walker,* 2006 OK 43, 157 P.3d 100. The practitioner should also make reference to federal cases, such as *Great Western Life & Annuity Insurance Company v. Knudson*, 534 U.S. 204, 210, 122 S.Ct. 708, 713 (2002) and *Sereboff v. Mid Atlantic Medical Services, Inc.*, 547 U.S. 356, 126 S. Ct. 1869, 164 L. Ed. 2d 612, *Alves v Silverado Foods*, 6 Fed. Appx. 694, 2001 WL 237314 (10th Cir., Okla., 2001); *Admin. Cmmte. of Wal-Mart Assoc. Health and Welfare Plan v Willard*, 302 F.Supp.2d 267 (D.Kan., 2004), aff'd 393 F.3d 1119 (10th Cir., 2004). Also see *Fields v Farmers Ins. Co.*, 18 F.3d 831 (10th Cir., Okla., 1994), although the interpretation of the policy language in *Fields* was disagreed with in *Youngblood* and *Reeds*.

Chapter 7: Medical Payments.

§7:2 Occupancy.

In *Walker v Farmers Ins. Co., Inc.*, 83 F.3d 349 (10th Cir. 1996) the Court had to deal with a long standing feud that erupted into gunfire. The insured was in his van when it was broadsided by a pickup driven by Perry Enloe. Wayne Enloe, Perry's father then stopped his truck, got a gun and began firing shots. The insured exited his van and ran down the road. He was felled by a bullet, and Wayne Enloe then fired a shot into his head, killing him. The insured surviving spouse made claim under the UM and the Med Pay portions of the Farmers policy. Regarding the Med Pay claim, the claimant argued that the insured was "alighting" from the vehicle when he was shot. However, the Tenth Circuit noted that the insured was well away from his car, and in the process of running down the road, when he was eventually shot. Therefore, they held that he was not "occupying" his vehicle at the time of his death.

§7:4 Payment of medical expenses. [New]

Quite often a medical provider will write off or reduce their full bill because of some contractual obligation (such as a Medicare agreement or the requirements of a health insurance plan. The question then becomes whether the med pay insured is entitled to recover the "full billed" amount of the bill, or the amount that the medical provider actually accepted for payment for services. In *Woodrich v Farmers Ins. Co.*, 405 F.Supp.2d 1276 (N.D. OK., 2004) the Court held that the auto insurer had no obligation under its Med Pay coverage to pay the amount of medical bills that had been written off by medical providers.

§7:11 -Subrogation.

In *Estes v American Fidelity Ins. Co.*, 2000 OK CIV APP 99, 11 P.3d 1263, the Court of Civil Appeals held that the anti-subrogation statute, 36 O.S. §6092, did not prevent the operation of an "other insurance" clause in a Medical Payments policy. Estes was a guest passenger in the Weddle vehicle and Weddle's Medical Payments insurer (Farmers) paid Estes medical bills. Farmers then subrogated against the tortfeasor's insurer, and recovered their payment. Estes then made a Medical Payments claim against his own insurer (Mercury) for payment for the same medical bills that Farmers had paid. The Court held that Mercury's "other insurance" clause made the Farmers policy primary, and that §6092 did not change this result, since the operation of Mercury's "other insurance" clause was not "subrogation" prohibited by §6092.

Settlement by insured with tortfeasor when Medical Payments insurer has given notice of its subrogation rights..

36 O.S. §6092 allows subrogation when the injured insured is a guest-passenger. It has long been held that an insured under a Medical Payments provision, who is on notice of the subrogation claim being asserted by the insurer, can not, by settlement and release, destroy the Medical Payments insurer's right to collect subrogation against the insured's recovery. *State Farm Fire & Cas. Ins. Co. v Farmers Ins. Exch.*, 1971 OK 120, 489 P.2d 480. The issue

was revisited in *Manokoune v State Farm Mut. Auto. Ins. Co.*, 2006 OK 74, 145 P.3d 1081. Equity Ins. made Medical Payments to its guest-passenger insured Vichai. Equity gave notice of its subrogation claim to the tortfeasor's insurer, State Farm, but gave no notice to Vichai. State Farm did not tell Vichai that Equity claimed a subrogation interest. Vichai settled with State Farm's insured, by friendly suit, and gave a draft to Vichai that included Equity's name. This was Vichai's first notice that Equity claimed a subrogation right that would diminish Vichai's settlement proceeds. Vichai filed suit against Equity and State Farm. The case turned on whether Equity had given proper notice of its subrogation rights to Vichai before the settlement. The Court held that "notice" could be actual or constructive. There was no evidence that Equity had given actual notice to Vichai, but Equity argued that Vichai had constructive notice of the terms of the policy by accepting benefits under the policy. However, the Court held that it was a question of fact whether Vichai had constructive notice, since Vichai was a guest passenger and had never seen the policy, and whether State Farm was obligated to tell Vichai what it knew about Equity's subrogation notice prior to settling with Vichai.

§7:15 Stacking.

The Court reiterated its conclusion that Medical Payments coverage does not "stack" in

Simpson v Farmers Ins. Co., 1999 OK 51, 981 P.2d 1262. Simpson had four vehicles insured with Farmers, each with Med Pay coverage. If stacked, the policies would total $17,000. However, Farmers would only pay $5,000 because the policies provided that in the event Farmers had issued more that one policy covering medical expenses, "the total amount payable among all such policies shall not exceed the limits provided by the single policy with the highest limits of liability." The insured claimed the right to stack the policies because there were four separate premiums paid. The Court noted that the "reasonable expectations doctrine" adopted in *Max True Plastering v U.S.F.&G.*, 1996 OK 28, 912 P.2d 861 (see §1:2 in the main volume) did not change the result. The Court said that it would not "engag[e] in wholesale rewriting of insurance policies" when the language of the polices was clear.

§7:17 Named Driver Exclusion.

The Supreme Court has determined that an auto Liability insurer is entitled to exclude named individuals from coverage by using a "named driver endorsement." See *Pierce v Oklahoma Property and Casualty Ins. Co.*, 1995 OK 78, 901 P.2d 819, discussed at §5:10 in the main volume. The holding in *Pierce* was applied to a Medical Payments provision in *Robinson v GEICO General Ins. Co.*, 1996 OK CIV APP 130, 928 P.2d 971. The GEICO policy contained a general "named driver exclusion" barring any coverage for a certain driver. The Court of Appeals held that this was valid and would apply to bar Medical Payments coverage for the named driver.

§7:20 Choice of law. [new]

The Court of Civil Appeals has held that the coverage of a Medical Payments policy is governed by the law of the state where the policy was issued. *In re Farmers Med-Pay Litigation*, 2010 OK CIV APP 12, 229 P.3d 551. The practitioner should bear in mind, however, that Oklahoma does regulate Medical Payments subrogation by statute, so the result may, or may not, be different if that were the issue.

Chapter 8: Property Coverages.

§8:25 The Measure of Damages. Limits of Liability; Actual cash value; repair; delay, etc.

§8:26 -In General

The Motor vehicle Total Loss Settlement statute. 36 O.S. §1250.8

This statute has gone through a couple of revisions since the publication of the main volume, the latest being in November, 2010. The practitioner should always review this statute to assure that the insurer is living up to its obligations regarding loss calculation and payment, cash settlement and junk titles. As in the main volume, we will provide the full text of the statute for review.

36 O.S. §1250.8 (after revisions found in 2010 Session Laws, Chap. 321).

A. If an insurance policy or insurance contract provides for the adjustment and settlement of first party motor vehicle total losses, on the basis of actual cash value or replacement with another of like kind and quality, one of the following methods shall apply:

1. An insurer may elect to offer a replacement motor vehicle which is a specific comparable motor vehicle available to the insured, with all applicable taxes, license fees, and other fees incident to the transfer of evidence of ownership of the motor vehicle paid, at no cost to the insured other than any deductible provided in the policy. The offer and any rejection thereof shall be documented in the claim file; or

2. An insurer may elect a cash settlement based upon the actual cost, less any deductible provided in the policy, to purchase a comparable motor vehicle, including all applicable taxes, license fees and other fees incident to a transfer of evidence of

ownership, or a comparable motor vehicle. Such cost may be determined by:

a. the cost of a comparable motor vehicle in the local market area when a comparable motor vehicle is currently or recently available in the prior ninety (90) days in the local market area,

b. one of two or more quotations obtained by an insurer from two or more qualified dealers located within the local market area when a comparable motor vehicle is not available in the local market area, or

c. the cost of a comparable motor vehicle as quoted in the latest edition of the National Automobile Dealers Association Official Used Car Guide or monthly edition of any other nationally recognized published guidebook.

B. If a first party motor vehicle total loss is settled on a basis which deviates from the methods described in subsection A of this section, the deviation shall be supported by documentation giving particulars of the condition of the motor vehicle. Any deductions from such cost, including, but not limited to, deduction for salvage, shall be measurable, discernible, itemized and specified as to dollar amount and shall be appropriate in amount. The basis for such settlement shall be fully explained to a first party claimant.

C. If liability for motor vehicle damages is reasonably clear, insurers shall not recommend that third party claimants make claims pursuant to the third party claimants' own policies solely to avoid paying claims pursuant to such insurer's insurance policy or insurance contract.

D. Insurers shall not require a claimant to travel unreasonably either to inspect a replacement motor vehicle, obtain a repair estimate or have the motor vehicle repaired at a specific repair shop.

E. Insurers shall, upon the request of a claimant, include the deductible of a first party claimant, if any, in subrogation demands. Subrogation recoveries shall be shared on a proportionate basis with a first party claimant, unless the deductible amount has been otherwise recovered. No deduction for expenses shall be made from a deductible recovery unless an outside attorney is retained to collect such recovery. The deduction shall then be made for only a pro rata share of the allocated loss adjustment expense.

F. If an insurer prepares an estimate of the cost of automobile repairs, such estimate shall be in an amount for which it reasonably may be expected that the damage can be repaired satisfactorily. An insurer shall give a copy of an estimate to a claimant and may furnish to the claimant the names of one or more conveniently located repair shops, if requested by the claimant.

G. If an amount claimed is reduced because of betterment or depreciation, all information for such reduction shall be contained in the claim file. Such deductions shall be itemized and specified as to dollar amount and shall be appropriate for the amount of deductions.

H. An insurer or its representative shall not require a claimant to obtain motor vehicle repairs at a specific repair facility. An insurer or its representative shall not require a claimant to obtain motor vehicle glass repair or replacement at a specific motor vehicle glass repair or replacement facility. An insurer shall fully and promptly pay for the cost of the motor vehicle repair services or products, less any applicable deductible amount payable according to the terms of the policy. The claimant shall be furnished an itemized priced statement of repairs by the repair facility at the time of acceptance of the repaired motor vehicle. Unless a cash settlement is made, if a claimant selects a motor vehicle repair or motor vehicle glass repair or replacement facility, the insurer shall provide payment to the facility or claimant based on a competitive price, as established by that insurer through market surveys or by the insured through competitive bids at the insured's option, to determine a fair and reasonable market price for similar services. Reasonable deviation from this market price is allowed based on the facts in each case.

I. An insurer shall not use as a basis for cash settlement with a first party claimant an amount which is less than the amount which an insurer would pay if repairs were made, other than in total loss situations, unless such amount is agreed to by the insured.

J. An insurer shall not force a claimant to execute a full settlement release in order to settle a property damage claim involving a personal injury.

K. All payment or satisfaction of a claim for a motor vehicle which has been transferred by title to the insurer shall be paid by check or draft, payable on demand.

L. In the event of payment of a total loss to a third party claimant, the insurer shall include any registered lienholder as copayee to the extent of the lienholder's interest.

M. As used in this section, "total loss" means that the vehicle repair costs plus the salvage value of the vehicle meets or exceeds the actual cash value of the motor vehicle prior to the loss, as provided in used automobile dealer guidebooks.

N. An insurer shall not offer a cash settlement as provided in paragraph 2 of subsection A of this section for the purchase of a comparable motor vehicle and then subsequently sell the motor vehicle which has been determined to be a total loss back to the claimant if the insurer has determined that the repair of the vehicle would not result in the vehicle being restored to operative condition as provided in Section 1111 of Title 47 of the Oklahoma Statutes unless the claimant specifies in writing or via an electronic signature that the claimant understands that the motor vehicle shall be titled as a "junked vehicle".

Oklahoma Automobile Insurance Law and Practice
2012 Supplement
TABLE OF CASES
References are to Sections

Admin. Cmmte. of Wal-Mart Assoc. Health and Welfare Plan v Willard, 302 F.Supp.2d 267 (D.Kan., 2004), aff'd 393 F.3d 1119 (10th Cir., 2004) - § 6:133

Air Liquide America Corp. v Continental Cas. Co., 217 F.3d 1272 (10th Cir. 2002) - § 2:25, 3:48, 4:45, 4:60

Alternative Medicine of Tulsa, Inc. v Cates, 2006 OK CIV APP 65, 136 P.3d 716 - § 5:10, 6:49

Alves v Silverado Foods, 6 Fed. Appx. 694, 2001 WL 237314 (10th Cir., Okla., 2001) - § 6:133

American Cas. Co. of Reading, PA v Health Care Indem. Co., 520 F.3d 1131 (10th Cir., Ok., 2008) - § 3:47

American Economy Ins. Co. v Bogdahn, 2004 OK 9, 89 P.3d 1051 - § 1:2, 2:18, 4:45, 6:32

Badillo v Mid Century Ins. Co., 2005 OK 48, 121 P.3d 1080 - § 4:81

Made in United States
North Haven, CT
04 November 2026

21760248R00108